In his readable book, *Roasting Karma*, Kirk Johnson vividly and with disarming candour, shares his seemingly unending health challenges and painful life experiences with readers who may rightly wonder how one man can survive them all.
—Professor Kofi Asare Opoku, Chairman, Kwabena Nketia Centre for Africana Studies, African University College of Communications, Accra, Ghana

As a spiritual man, I can relate to *Roasting Karma*. Do unto others as you would have them do unto you. When we don't follow that philosophy, there's a price to pay. Kirk paid his dues!
—Tiger Jeet Singh Jr., WWE Wrestling Champion, President, Tiger Jeet Singh Foundation

Roasting Karma takes you deep into the mind of the author as he searches for truth. Join Kirk on his journey to self-realization and you may find yourself arriving there, too!
—Dorothy McLeod, Founder/Director; Jamaica Cultural Alliance

In *Roasting Karma*, Kirk demonstrates the steps to WAKE UP from this illusory life, same old patterns, and begin seeing things the way they truly are. This timely story of self-transformation helps us to battle onward during the days of uncertainty. It is wonderful to read a story of awakening when so many are still asleep. Your soul will light up with each turn of the page.
—April Tribe Giauque, author of *Pinpoints of Light* & *Out of Darkness*

In these difficult times, we are all looking for examples to help us. This is a compelling story of how one man copes with all that karma throws his way. *Roasting Karma* is truly a story for our time.
—Robert C. Paehlke, Emeritus Professor of Environmental and Resource Studies and Political Science, Trent University

Stop repeating the same old patterns! Kirk shows us the steps to wake up from this illusory life and begin seeing things the way they truly are. The time is now!
—Fay Thompson, author of *So Help Me God*

This book provides life lessons on how to conquer past hurts and move into a place of peace.
—Kary Oberbrunner, author of *Your Secret Name* and *Elixir Project*

I've known Kirk for many years. He has been a friend, business partner, mentor, and healer to me. Especially through my difficult journey with the loss of my wife, Janis, to a rare cancer. No matter what is happening, he always manages to stay calm. I refer to him fondly as "Morpheus" from *The Matrix* movie series. That's the wisdom and peace of meditation shining through. He clearly sees the matrix for what it is, and he's always *Roasting Karma*.
— Dr. Doug Lukinuk, BSc DC, CEO PTBO Chiro Inc., CEO Arc of Life Inc.

ROASTING KARMA

To Karen,

When good things happen, it's easy to be peaceful and happy. When bad things happen, it's just as easy to be peaceful and happy — if we choose to be.

Be the example!

ROASTING KARMA

Awaken From Illusion, Take Responsibility for Your Past Actions, and Create a Life That Is Truly Free

By: Kirk A. Johnson

HEALING DIGEST
PUBLISHING

Published by Healing Digest Publishing
808 Commerce Park Drive, Unit 62495
Ogdensburg, NY, 13669-2208
www.HealingDigest.com

Identifiers:
Library of Congress Control Number: 2020911047
ISBN: 978-0-578-71194-2 (paperback)
ISBN: 978-0-578-71195-9 (hardback)
ISBN: 978-0-578-71196-6 (e-book)

Available in paperback, hardback, e-book, and audiobook

Any Internet addresses (websites, blogs, etc.) and telephone numbers printed in this book are offered as a resource. They are not intended in any way to be or imply an endorsement by Healing Digest Publishing, nor does Healing Digest Publishing vouch for the content of these sites and numbers for the life of this book.

Some names and identifying details have been changed to protect the privacy of individuals.

Cover design by Debbie O'Byrne
Interior design by JetLaunch
Author photos by Owen Nabuurs

DEDICATION

Roasting Karma is dedicated to the anonymous souls who lost their lives, who allowed me to live. Two hearts and a kidney—three angels forever watching over me.
Namasté

TABLE OF CONTENTS

INTRODUCTION

This book is my gift to you, the reader. After becoming very ill, I lay in a hospital bed wondering, "What service could I perform for mankind that would cause God to keep me around?" He answered. God told me that if I could use my life of suffering and keys to survival as an example for others to follow, a life like that would be worth saving. That was our pact, and the contents of this book is the product of our collaboration.

I don't consider myself a religious man—more SBNR (spiritual but not religious). When I was young, however, my parents took me to a Baptist Church. While they went into the big hall, my sisters and I went with a Sunday-school teacher, to Bible study. I enjoyed the morally-minded stories: Daniel in the Lion's Den, Joseph and the Coat of Many Colors, Samson and Delilah, and more. I could even rattle off, by rote, the books of the Bible, both the Old and the New Testament. Every Christmas, I loved watching the Ten Commandments: the original one with Yul Brynner and Charlton Heston. I was always a bit shaken when Moses went up into the mountains and God spoke to him through a burning bush, or when God scorched the commandments into stone—with fire. Later in life, I realized it wasn't fear I sensed about the burning bush, but a powerful reverence for God. However, as my parents fell away from the weekly Sunday church ritual, so did I. Still craving that reverence for God, yet finding no solutions in any church, I let go of my search. I struggled to believe that the only way I could have a relationship with God was having to first pass through a preacher or priest; neither of which was I certain had their own true relationship with God. Tantamount to the blind leading the blind. I could no longer suffer religion.

Once I hit my thirties, I had all but forgotten about my search for Spirit. In fact, I was pretty sure I could do without it. Unfortunately, spirituality is something we need to balance out the mental and physical aspects of ourselves. It's around this period of life (thirties and onward) that we are either drawn to it, or we get the good ole shove in the back. At 32 years of age, I got my shove and it changed my life forever. Join me, as I take you on my roller-coaster journey to bring my life back into balance. Maybe you'll see yourself in some of the pages, and if you do, hopefully you'll find your way to some of the same solutions as I did.

Why call the book *Roasting Karma*? After becoming ill, my life changed completely. The seriousness of the illnesses precluded me from returning to the life I had enjoyed until then. I went from an intelligent, athletic, and decent-looking guy—with swagger—to a weak, fearful, and at times, frail individual. I came to understand that spirituality was the missing key in my life. Once I began to study and understand spirituality, I realized what was happening to me was payback for things I had done, and choices I had made in the past. I came to understand that this payback was known as the *Universal Law of Karma*.

Karma is the law of action or cosmic justice, based upon cause and effect. Your every act, good or bad, has a specific effect on your life. The effects of actions in this life remain lodged in the subconsciousness; those brought over from past existences are hidden in the superconsciousness[i], ready like seeds to germinate under the influence of a suitable environment. Karma decrees that as one sows, so must he inevitably reap.[ii]

At first this worried me, especially knowing I hadn't always done good deeds in this life; not to mention deeds I had done in previous lives that I no longer remembered. Typically, in life, whenever there is a problem, human beings are quick to find someone else to blame. The *blame game* is a fruitless undertaking and only leads to sadness, anger, or guilt, for all parties involved— a lose-lose situation. Conversely, when we take responsibility for our actions, and then forgive ourselves, we cauterize those negative emotions and reveal a path through which happiness can flourish—win-win!

Understanding that blaming someone else for my karmic debts caused negative emotions, whereas accepting my karmic debts could produce happiness, I wondered what would happen if I called for *all of my karma* to come at once? Further study indicated that it is our unpaid karma that keeps us tied to the wheel of rebirth: reincarnation or *samsara*. We must be born, live, die, and then be reborn again and again—sometimes millions of incarnations— until we repay our karmic debt. Once we repay our karmic debt, we free ourselves from the wheel of rebirth and are free to remain alongside God; be one with him and know him. "He who overcomes, I will make him a pillar in the temple of my God, and he shall go out no more."[iii]

That's what I wanted. This life seemed all too familiar to me, like I had been here many times before. I was done. I needed a legitimate way out. I prayed for all my karma to be given to me... and it was. Of course, I was totally unaware of the measure of the bill I still had to pay. In searching for a way to ease the debt, I came across a yogic meditation practice taught by Paramahansa Yogananda called Kriya yoga. Yogananda stated that, "Since all effects or seeds of our past actions, our karma, can be destroyed by *roasting* them in the fire of meditation, concentration, the light of superconsciousness, and right actions, there is no such thing as fate. You make your own destiny. God has given you independence, and you are free to shut out his power or let it in."

Not only did Yogananda teach me how to roast karma through meditation, alignment with him, a guru-avatar, takes away a portion of the karma I would have suffered all on my own. I take 25% of my karma, the guru takes 25%, and 50% is the grace of God. That's a portion I can handle and that is why I make the supreme effort, day and night, to keep on *Roasting Karma!*

PART I

AWAKENING

1997 - 1999

1

WALK-IN, BUT YOU CAN'T WALK OUT!

When we are no longer able to change a situation, we are challenged to change ourselves.

~ Viktor Frankl

I stood there transfixed, my hand on the doorknob. Why couldn't I pass through the door I had entered a mere twenty minutes ago? Perhaps it was the news I had just received from the doctor. He was still sitting behind me, watching me pause before I walked out the door. The news he gave me was just words, yet somehow those words paralyzed me. I felt a cold chill moving from the top of my head down to my feet. The words played again and again in my head, deafening me to all other noise. How did it ever come to this?

I had woken up that day in Toronto at my mother's house. The evening before, I'd made the long two-and-a-half-hour drive from my home in Peterborough, Ontario, to pick up my son Travis in Kitchener. Then, we made the hour-and-fifteen-minute drive to my mother's place. Toronto was a convenient halfway point on the backend of those five-hour round trips from Peterborough to Kitchener and back. On this particular June weekend in1997, there was an added benefit: it was Travis's eighth birthday, and I was taking him to Sega City in Mississauga, just outside Toronto. Travis loved video games, and Sega City had them all—even the interactive ones that you could ride, climb on, and fly in. I wanted to do something special for him, especially since we didn't see each other that often. (Due to the distance between us, I only saw him every three weeks.) We had breakfast at my mom's place and headed out for the day.

As we drove, I could notice my body swaying with every heartbeat—back and forth, like a pendulum. This was the norm now, as I had noticed it about three months ago. I'm not sure why I chose that day, but on the way back from Sega City, I asked Travis if he'd mind stopping at the walk-in clinic in the mall down the street from my mother's apartment. Having spent the last three hours playing every interactive video game imaginable, as well as a round of mini golf, he was cool with it—so in we went.

After checking in with the receptionist, we sat in the waiting area. An older black lady seated beside me leaned over and gave me a little pamphlet to read. It was entitled *The Daily Word*. From the outside looking in, this may not have seemed like anything unusual. What *was* unusual was that I had seen these little pamphlets for years. My mother would give them to me, and each time she did, I'd tell her, "Mom, stop giving me this crap—I'm not into it!" But this time, I read the pamphlet from cover to cover. The gist of the message was to contact your inner power as a guide to living your daily life...whatever that meant.

Not long after I read the pamphlet, my name was called. I made my way past the reception desk and into an examination room. A doctor came in and asked me why I was there. I explained the rocking, and that I'd also been having quite a few headaches lately. The doctor did his stethoscope thing and listened to my chest, in front and in the back. Then he wrapped an inflatable cuff around my upper arm, pumped it up, and slowly let the air out. He watched the pressure gauge while listening with his stethoscope, its head placed at the inside of my elbow. Then, as if he wasn't sure of the result the first time, he repeated the process. He then asked me to remove my shirt: he was requesting an electrocardiogram (or ECG). Shortly thereafter, a technician came in and applied a bunch of sticky, two-inch, round, spongy paper circles with little metal nipples to my chest, then attached alligator clips to the metal nipples with long colored wire leads that fed back to a machine. "Don't move please," he said. The technician ran the machine for a few seconds, and then it made a printout. He said, "Thank you," and left the room.

The doctor returned with a concerned look on his face and began asking questions about my life: "What type of work do you do?" "Are you in a relationship?" "What do you do in your spare time?" and "How long have you been experiencing these conditions?" I gave him a brief rundown of my life and told him that I'd been experiencing these symptoms for about three months. It was then that he looked me square in the eye and said those dreaded words, prefaced by the ever-respectful *Mr. Johnson*: "Your blood pressure is dangerously high: 190/140. You need to go to the hospital in an ambulance immediately. With a blood pressure like that, it would be malpractice to let you walk out of here."

My first response was amazement and shock, mixed with a hint of anger. I immediately retorted, "There is no way I'm leaving here in an ambulance. It's my son's birthday and there's no way I'm going to let him see me go out like that. I'm perfectly fine. I can drop my son off at my mom's place, then head over to the hospital to get fully checked out."

The doctor was silent for a moment, then capitulated and submitted, "While it is not my preference, I suppose that since you have been experiencing these symptoms for three months now, another few hours won't make that much of a difference."

Disregarding the severity of the moment yet filled with pride to have won that little battle, I stood up, turned on my heels, and headed for the door. That's when it hit me. A little voice inside was telling me, "You don't know what's on the other side of that door." Of course, that was silly. I knew exactly what was on the other side of that door—the reception area, a pile of people, and my son. The little voice wasn't speaking literally, but metaphorically, and what was on the other side of that door was *a big unknown*. For months now, I'd been walking around with a life-threatening physical problem and didn't know it. Yes, there were little signs here and there, but individually they meant nothing. Now, that I knew what those little signs added up to, it meant everything. Panic hit, and thoughts of something bad happening while I was driving with my son made it all seem a little too real. All this foreboding was enough for me to change my mind and listen to the advice of the doctor. Except for that stupid pride, that was the last hurdle. Finally, measuring the preponderance of fear against the stupid, ego-driven pride, I turned away from the door and sat back down with the doctor.

A rush of emotion came over me. I wasn't sure if it was about finding out that I was ill, the safety of my son, an unknown future, or having to back down from a fight. Maybe it was a mixture of it all? Perhaps there was a middle-ground solution? I had another idea and laid it out before the doctor: "How about if I call my mother and explain the situation to her. She lives close by and could quickly come and pick up my son. Then, I could make my way over to the hospital, without endangering the life of my boy." He agreed. I called my mother and she was on her way.

My mother, Joy, as she was commonly known amongst friends and family, was very good under pressure. I suppose all mothers are when it comes to their children, but Joy was especially good in *triage* situations. She showed up with a couple of her friends in tow, Patience and Darlene. They would take Travis home to their place and my mother would drive me to the emergency department at the nearest hospital. This seemed like a plan and was satisfactory to the doctor. Time to execute!

My mother drove me to East York General Hospital and, on advice from the clinic doctor, I was quickly rushed through processing and was now before the emergency doctor. He asked me all the same questions, so I replied in kind: "I'm a business tax auditor with Revenue Canada. I'm also enrolled in the Certified General Accountants of Ontario (CGA) program working towards my accounting designation while, at the same time, completing a business degree through distance education. I have to do it together because I'm also applying for a position as a *corporate* tax auditor and need the credentials in order to be considered. The tax department has allowed me to write the competition even though I haven't achieved those credentials and if I'm successful in the position, I could keep it—if I achieve the credentials by the time the competition outcome gets posted. (Just a little pressure!) I'm also the president of our tax union local and was elected to the National Bargaining Committee that is currently in sessions with the Treasury Board of Canada. Since the bargaining sessions are in Ottawa. I had to schedule to write some of my CGA exams in Ottawa, in the middle of the bargaining process." (Just a little more pressure!)

The emergency room (ER) doctor looked at me with raised eyebrows and made the obvious comment, "You are under a lot of stress for a guy that's only thirty-two. Let's see if we can't bring that blood pressure down." I removed my shirt and put on one of those customary, light blue, tie-in-the-back gowns and lay down on a stretcher. Working with the doctor was a young assistant, and he came over to apply those round stickers again, except this time they were attached to a monitor to keep track of my vital signs. He also inserted an intravenous needle, with a line that was attached to a bag of fluid.

What happened next, I will never forget for the rest of my life. As I lay on my back, faceup on the table, (I was holding my mother's hand as she looked down upon me, consoling me, telling me everything would be okay) I noticed the young assistant injecting something into the intravenous line. A warm feeling began emanating from my solar plexus. At first this feeling was very mild, but then it began to get stronger—and stronger. If I were a lake, it would be as if someone dropped a stone in the center of me and the circular ripples began moving outward to encompass my entire body of water. Immediately, I knew something was wrong. It's as if my life force were preparing to leave my body; and while I had never experienced that sensation before, that's exactly what I imagined it would feel like. Now the warmth was turning into fear, and someone was turning the thermostat way up. At that point, I squeezed my mother's hand and told her, "Something is wrong! Something is really wrong!"

Right then, *Triage Joy* went into action. She shouted to the doctor, "There is a problem here! I AM A NURSE! My son is in trouble!" In truth, my mother is not a nurse, but she definitely knows how to get some attention. The emergency doctor quickly made his way across the room, and upon seeing what was happening, pushed the assistant out of the way and took control of the situation. Within a few moments, I could feel the warmth subsiding and my body returning to normal. At that time, nothing more was said about what happened, or why; but I had a gut feeling I'd dodged a bullet—big time! I was later stabilized, officially admitted to the hospital, and left the emergency room.

I'd never been sick as an adult, and so this experience was all new to me. As a child, I had acute appendicitis resulting in my appendix being removed, and later, a severe bout of gastroenteritis. I couldn't help but notice, though, that both of those childhood maladies had been pushed to the extreme before being attended to. Now here I was again, with very high blood pressure that needed to be addressed and controlled quickly. As a kid, you leave everything up to your parents and the doctors, and the whole experience is resolved with very little question. However, as an adult, you take a little more interest in what's going on: the various tests, procedures and examinations, what they are for, and why you need them. We were going through a process of elimination. First off, I recalled hearing ramblings about *ischemic changes* in my heart that were noticed on the ECGs. The result of those ramblings was a Nitro patch. My *Spidey sense* was telling me they were barking up the wrong tree. It was explained to me that the Nitro patch was used to open the blood pathways and prevent another heart attack. "Another heart attack!" I mused, "I've never experienced a heart attack?" but apparently the test results indicated that I may have had an angina attack that went unnoticed. "Hmmm... unnoticed angina attack eh?" I thought, "Not bloody likely!" All I knew was that the Nitro patch was giving me a splitting headache. I'm calling that elimination number one!

Finally, they realized there had been no heart attack and I, thankfully, got off the nitroglycerin. Next, they informed me that the kidneys did many jobs: like balancing minerals and fluids in the body; they also create an enzyme called renin that can affect blood pressure throughout the body. If there is some problem with the kidneys, it could affect the renin production and, ultimately, the blood pressure. They were asking me if I would submit to an open biopsy of my kidney. Of course, I said "Yes." In hindsight though, I now know that a biopsy of the kidney can be done laparoscopically, in which three to five small incisions are made, and a magnifying telescope is used along with long, thin surgical instruments that could have biopsied the kidney with very little trauma. The open biopsy is about a five-inch incision just below and along the side of the ribcage, and the rehab is very painful. If I recall correctly, the story was that I'd been given blood thinners, which made laparoscopic surgery much riskier for bleeding complications; the open biopsy was the only way to go. My mom still asserts that the reason for the open biopsy was to *harvest one of my kidneys*. We all still laugh about that one. She was always leery about the medical profession.

After leaving the emergency ward, I was bounced all over the hospital running tests. The only constant was that there were chicks aplenty! Hot nurses and doctors were around every corner. You'd think with what I was going through, my focus would be on my health. Don't get me wrong, it was, but I'm not a blind man and was conscious of the new terrain. I suppose since I was in the hospital, I should deal with *all* my afflictions. My lifelong preoccupation with members of the opposite sex could be considered an ailment—and those who knew me might say it was a full-blown disease. At thirty-two, I still had it goin' on, so to speak—and so the hunt continued. Got to address that soon.

One of the days of my stay, the ER doctor came to see me. He shared his thoughts that, "I was just the emergency doctor on call that day, and I don't usually come to visit patients who pass through the emergency ward, but for some reason I just had to come and see you. You're such a young guy, and you have so much on your plate. You know…We almost lost you in the ER that day." He may have said something else, but after his last sentence it was as if he wasn't even there anymore. My mind dwelled on those words, "We almost lost you in the ER that day." The words echoed through me for some time. I knew something was wrong, but having never experienced anything like that before, I wasn't sure. Now, I was! My mind ran to *death*—and how quickly it could come. One moment you're there, feel a little warmth in the chest, and the next minute you're gone. Wham! Bam! Thank you, ma'am! Life is fleeting. Thank God my mother was there with me. She may have saved my life.

2

HOODOO YOU THINK YOU ARE?

The soul that is without suffering does not feel the need of knowing the ultimate cause of knowing the universe. Sickness, grief, hardships, etc., are all indispensable elements in the spiritual ascent.

~ Sri Anandamayi Ma

The hospital was a busy place. There was always a lot of hustle and bustle. As I lay on the bed in the single-occupant room I'd been given, I listened to the omnipresent buzz of the hallways. I overheard a man who seemed irate that he was being asked to leave the hospital. I heard the nurses at the station telling him that he was better now and there was no reason for him to stay. I'm not sure how I knew, but I could tell he was homeless and did not want to go back out onto the street after whatever treatment he had received. He begged to stay but the nurses' hands were tied. All I could think was, "I hope I'm not in the room he just got booted out of! I'm not in any kind of shape for a donnybrook." In the end, they had to call security, as well as the police, to take care of him. I myself couldn't wait to get out of the hospital—just not that way! It's funny how life shuffles the deck: the only hand you get is the one you are dealt. While you can trade in a few cards, sometimes your hand improves, sometimes it just makes things worse.

When one thinks of the hospital staff, the first people who come to mind are often the nurses and doctors, but there are a whole host of people necessary to run the day-to-day operations. My favorites were always the orderlies and assistants. Why? To me, they were always more genuine and authentic—probably because they had nothing to prove. There was a black woman of Caribbean descent that came in to check my room, sweep, and empty the trash. She looked around as she came near, leaned in, and whispered to me, "You shouldn't be here!"

"Okay?" I thought. "If what had been happening the last few days wasn't enough to make my hair stand on end, this was it." "What do you mean I shouldn't be here?" I asked.

She just shook her head and repeated the same words "You shouldn't be here." She looked around again. I'm not sure what she was looking for, but I imagine she was just making sure there were no doctors or nurses listening. She whispered again, "I'm going to bring you the number of a woman to call. She knows things. She will explain everything." Then she left the room.

I was puzzled by this interaction and wondered what the woman meant. While I wasn't a religious man, I had seen enough movies about voodoo, hoodoo, psychics, and rituals to venture a guess about what this woman was suggesting, and I must say it intrigued me. I couldn't wait for her to come back. She returned a short while later with a phone number on a card and a plug-in phone for me to use. She instructed me on what time I should call, which would be later that evening, and then she left again. At the prearranged time, I made the call. The whole event seemed so strange and macabre, and the conversation with this woman was no different. When I dialed the number, it rang and an elderly, confident, yet mysterious, voice answered the phone. I gave my name and she seemed to know why I was calling. I mentioned that, "The lady in the hospital told me I wasn't supposed to be here and gave me your number. Can you tell me what she is talking about?"

The mysterious voice replied, "Yes, but first I need to find you."

"Find me? What the heck does that mean?" I wondered. I waited for her to continue.

The voice returned a few moments later and mused, "This is strange, I cannot find you. This is very strange. It's like you are no longer with us. It looks like you are going to have to moan it out. Yes, you are going to have to moan it out. That is all I can tell you. You are going to have to moan it out!"

As this was a strange occurrence, and my comfort level was not at its highest during this conversation, I accepted the fact that it was all she could tell me. "Thank you, goodbye," I said. A few moments later my head came out of the clouds. I wondered why I didn't ask her what, "you're going to have to moan it out," meant. As fate would have it, I would soon find out.

PAIN! After the open kidney biopsy, that's all I can remember—pain! Now I'm a pretty tough guy. I played American football in high school and university and suffered torn up knuckles, stitches in multiple places, severe bruising, charley horses, and I had my bell rung a few times, but this was another animal altogether. They went in on my right side, just below the rib line, and made an incision about six inches long. It was all bandaged up, but when the nurses came to change the dressing, I could see they used staples to close the wound. I had heard about such things but had never experienced it myself. It wasn't the incision or the staples that were giving me discomfort, it was the fact that they had cut through the lateral muscle groupings. From the pain I was feeling, these muscles were involved in every movement I made. It wasn't comfortable to lay on my back nor on my right side, obviously. All that was left was to lay on my left side. Sure, they gave me drugs to numb the pain, but it wasn't touching it, as far as I was concerned. All I could do was lay there on my side; I pulled my knees up toward my chest and assumed the fetal position. For a grown man, it truly felt like I was reverting back to an infant—and the only comfort I could engender was to moan.

I moaned so much it became just like breathing. Somehow that low-pitched, murmuring buzz was soothing—and I'm not sure whether it was soothing to the wound itself, or to my body and mind as a whole. Was I feeling sorry for myself? Yes, absolutely! And I didn't care what anybody thought about it. Was I *moaning it out*? Maybe I was, but there was no instruction manual; no way of knowing whether I was doing the hoodoo lady's version of moaning at all. Only time would tell.

As I lay in the fetal posture, with my back to the door facing the window, I looked out at the blue sky and began to wonder why this was all happening to me. I didn't think I was that bad of a person; I never killed anyone, I wasn't a bank robber, and I earned my living honestly. A tear rolled down the bridge of my nose and onto the pillow. Just then, I felt a hand touch my shoulder. Immersed in self-pity, I didn't hear anyone enter the room. I immediately rolled over, albeit gingerly, to see who had come in behind me, and to my surprise no one was there. "Whoa! What the...?"

"So what?" I thought. "On top of everything I'm going through, I'm also going nuts?" I definitely felt a hand on my shoulder. There was no doubt in my mind. "What, or who, could it have been?" I searched my mind for all plausible explanations and could come up with none—save one: "Was it...an Angel?" I had heard about such things, and probably watched similar events happen on television, and in movies, but I never really gave it much thought. "Was it possible?" I wondered "Could something like this actually be happening to me? Why not?" The thought of it all was quite comforting. "Touched on the shoulder by an Angel." Pretty cliché if you ask me, but hey... I can roll with it! I closed my eyes and went to sleep.

The next day, the surgeon came to give me his findings. I was hoping for some resolution to this mess, so I listened intently to the report. He stated, "When we biopsied the kidney, the glomeruli, which are the parts of the kidney that filter waste and fluids from the body, were damaged. It looked as though they had been eaten away by something. In fact, it looked very similar to tissue under an immune attack. As a result, we're ordering an HIV test." He went on to say some other things, including the fact that I was getting discharged. He continued with instructions on when to return to have the staples removed, but once again my ears were deaf to his words, given the news I had just received.

"Fuuuck! Did not see that coming!" I thought to myself. "As if I didn't have enough to worry about." Historically, right around this time, HIV and AIDS were making news worldwide. People were dying from it left, right, and center. I was pretty sure that I was not HIV positive, but pretty sure wasn't enough to stop me from worrying. You must remember that I grew up in the age before condoms were invented. Okay, you got me there. Yes, they had been invented but very few people used them, and I was not one of the very few. When I was in my teens, and began sowing my oats, there was no big fear of HIV—just old-fashioned STDs—nothing a little tetracycline couldn't fix. And besides, I had been tested once or twice before and the results were always negative. Still...I had been a bit of a hound, and back then, you never knew what surprise you'd find inside the Cracker Jack box! I'd rolled the dice way too many times, and now it was coming back to haunt me.

Arrangements were made to get Travis back home to Kitchener, and I was heading to my mother's apartment for convalescence. "So many things to do!" I worried to myself. I needed to contact work to let them know that I wouldn't be coming in for a while and give them a bit of an update as to what was going on. I also needed to contact a girl I had just met, Lorie Masterson. We were supposed to be getting together, and I didn't want her to think that I was no longer interested. Priorities, priorities! Yet, those checklist items seemed small in comparison to the worry and fear that I was experiencing. In the back of my mind, I was also a little concerned about my present accommodations. Don't get me wrong, I loved my mother, but from time to time she could be somewhat volatile in certain situations. A little bit of an *itchy trigger finger* you could say—you just never knew when it could go off!

My mother had a two-bedroom apartment on the 14th floor of a building in the Thorncliffe Park, East York area of Toronto. I had the bedroom closest to the kitchen, the guest room. The simple act of walking was exhausting; I lay down on the bed in the guest room. The pain from the surgery was no longer as intense as it had been in the hospital. The oxycodone seemed to be doing its job, but it wasn't pain I was concerned with. My mind was stuck on the HIV threat. Forget about high blood pressure, the possibilities of angina attacks, kidney problems; they all paled in comparison with full-blown HIV and AIDS—those babies were killers. "Why had I been so foolish in the past. I should have taken better precautions," I chastised. All the excuses for not wearing a condom—reduced sensation, coitus interruptus, remembering to always have one, the embarrassment of the purchase process, as well as the cost, and on—seemed insignificant compared to what I now faced. I was possessed by worry and fear.

Then something bizarre happened—like an episode right out of *The Twilight Zone*! As I lay in bed, bemoaning my situation, I soon tired and closed my eyes to get some rest. To my astonishment, I beheld a magnificent entity standing before me! How was this possible? When I say the entity was standing before me, in all actuality it was really standing in front of my closed eyelids. My first reaction was fright! I quickly popped my eyes open and thought "What the heck is going on? Did I really see what I thought I saw? Maybe it was just a hallucination. After all, I just had some serious surgery and was still taking painkillers." I had to check. I closed my eyes again, and there it was, larger-than-life, in bright effulgent colors: it was a very tall being, wearing a full-length, hooded, gown-like robe, much like something a monk would wear. Its arms were crossed in front of its chest and in one hand was a scythe and in the other a scepter with a tassel on the end.

"What did this all mean?" I thought. "Why was it here?" I looked for signs of whether this was a beneficent or malevolent being. My eyes were drawn to the head area, which remained hooded, such that the face was in shadow. The fear in me, coupled with the fact that I had never encountered anything like this before, caused me to interpret the hooded visage as belonging to something malevolent, and so I open my eyes quickly, once again. I looked up as if in prayer and said silently, "I'm not ready for this." I closed my eyes once again, and it was gone.

I lay there contemplating what had just happened and surmised that it was either the Angel of Mercy, or the Angel of Death. I suppose, if it was the Angel of Mercy, I should have tried to communicate with it in some way. All things considered, and not being much of a gambling man, if it was the Angel of Death, there was no way I wanted to delay. I hedged my bet; I asked for it to go away. My mind vacillated as to whether I had done the right thing. There were pros and cons for each side of the equation. Given the past weekend's events, the high blood pressure, almost losing my life, the open biopsy, and the HIV scare, there were more than enough reasons for it to be the Angel of Death. The scythe—essentially a sharp sword shaped like a hook—didn't help any. Then my mind wandered back to the touch on the shoulder I received while lying in the hospital bed. That touch was not frightening at all, to the contrary, it was very comforting. "Perhaps it was that same angel coming to tell me that everything would be okay. I'll try to hang onto that."

I got up and wandered around my mother's apartment for a while, and then it happened. Remember that itchy trigger finger I told you about? Well, it flinched! We were discussing something about our family history that might have been germane to the doctors, but when the doctor had asked about our history, my mother held it back. This really irritated me and so we got right into it. Normally, I enjoy a good debate, but I was damaged and exhausted, and I knew how these things always went. My mother would never back down even if she was wrong and neither would I, but today I just didn't have the energy to fight a battle, the outcome of which would be meaningless.

It could've been the fact that my mother was raised alongside five brothers that made her fight so fiercely, but I knew it wasn't that. My mother married my father, Welsey Johnson (Well-zee), when she was very young. She was also the daughter of a police inspector in Jamaica and lived under heavy rules in her childhood household. There seemed to be a transference of that authority from her father to her husband, and as with many relationships back in those days, obedience of the wife was paramount. Further to that, my father was a very shrewd businessman and had some manipulative tendencies that carried over into the relationship. He called the shots, and my mother followed. From what I recalled, everything was hunky-dory for many years until my father overleveraged himself with land, properties, and businesses. He needed my mother to sign off on various paperwork, sight unseen. One day, she simply had enough and refused. War ensued, and shortly after that my mother became tired and depressed. Seeing his opportunity, my father tried to have my mother committed in order to take control of the family finances. But having someone committed is no easy task. The person you're trying to commit must exhibit real psychological dysfunction, which my mother simply did not. The doctors knew she didn't need to be there and called my dad to come and pick her up. He wouldn't. That was the last straw. My mother opened her eyes for the first time, as an adult! Ever since then, right or wrong, she's never backed down from anything.

So, now you know what I faced that night. Sometimes, these altercations would ramp themselves up to a point where things were said that should never be said. It seemed like she was still fighting my father, although they'd been divorced for 20 years. She'd get that look in her eyes that she had with him near the end. I knew where this was all heading, and I just couldn't go there. By now, I was getting emotional. Way too many things had recently happened to me in a very short period. I may not have had very long to live, so I decided to leave; but before I did, I was going to get a few things off my chest.

"Mom, I gotta get out of here. I can't stay here with you," I said. "Sometimes you act crazy, and I just can't tell if it's an act or if you really are crazy!" I went on to rehash the events of a weekend my sisters and I spent at my mother's place, recently.

She lost it then, too. It was so important for her to be right, or to have her own way, that she didn't care who got trampled in the process. I didn't even know where I was going to go, but I had credit cards and plenty of room for purchases. I was in no shape to be wandering the streets looking for hotels, but I just couldn't handle the stress of events; I had no choice.

I went to my room to grab my things and headed for the door. As I was moving toward the door, I heard something unexpected: a sweet, soft voice called out to me and said "son, I don't want you to go." The voice stopped me dead in my tracks. I don't know if my mother had ever addressed me in that voice before, and it immediately disarmed me. My mother came toward me, put her arms around me, and directed me back to the couch in the living room. We both sat down, she held my head in her lap, and I began to cry. Tears flowed like the river Ganges and continued for some time. My mother and I had a real heart-to-heart talk. Seems no one ever told her that she came across as being crazy. Maybe it was that, or maybe it was just the thought of losing her son that broke the protective barrier she had put up since leaving my father. Who knows? Something happened between my mom and I that night. Something very special. Something I will never forget. Ever since then, my mother and I have had an open, truthful, and loving relationship. We also mutually agreed to call a spade a spade, moving forward.

3

BOOKS IN-STORE

Life will give you whatever experience is most helpful for the evolution of your consciousness. How do you know this is the experience you need? Because this is the experience you are having at the moment.

~ Eckhart Tolle

Kofi Annan said, "Literacy is a bridge from misery to hope," and I hoped to learn all I could about my misery. The next day, I realized I was in the right place; the personal issues were out of the way. My mother had been dabbling in metaphysics for many years. Metaphysics is the study of why we're here—how we got here, and what is the purpose of being here. She might have been well advanced in metaphysics if it weren't for a bad experience she had with my dad's brother, Rupert Hayle, who was highly advanced in the field. She wasn't ready for what he was trying to show her, and she became frightened and backed away from those studies. Now, she was involved with the Unity Church, a quasi-Christian-based nondenominational church more focused on spiritual concepts than religious dogmas; the same folks that produced the *Daily Word*.

Given the strange occurrences I had recently experienced, my mother was the perfect person to talk to about it. I relayed the story about the mysterious psychic woman and her advice to, "moan it out," and the touch on the shoulder while in the hospital bed, but I held my tongue when it came to the hooded, angelic apparition. Something told me I should keep that one to myself. Over time, my mother had accumulated a small library on spiritual topics such as meditation, channeling, ESP, personal growth, and spiritual growth. This was a great place to start. Something had changed inside me and opened a part of me that I had either avoided, or suppressed, for 32 years. My life was on the edge, and I needed to try to understand why. If I could understand how this life worked, I could do a much better job of surviving it. Game on!

The first book I read was the *Art of Meditation* by Joel Goldsmith. This copy was a small, dark blue, hardcover edition of 160 pages, which I burned through in a day. For most people, that wouldn't be much of an achievement, but I, historically, was not a big reader. I rarely read for enjoyment, mostly to learn something; this stuff fell into that category. Like a sponge, I began soaking up all the spiritual and metaphysical literature I could find. I also noticed, however, that it was important to put into practice what you are reading as the personal growth would not come simply by reading alone. As a result, I put Goldsmith's techniques to the test and began a simple meditation regimen to see what results I would get. At first, it was difficult trying to get all the thoughts that were running through my head to slow down, even for a few minutes. "This is going to take time," I thought, so I focused my readings on things I could do. There was a book on ESP (extrasensory perception) that taught you how to call out to a person in the distance who was turned in the opposite direction. You would focus your mind on their medulla oblongata—the point at the back of the skull where it meets the spine—and call out their name, mutely, in your mind. If you did that strongly enough, they would turn around to look to see who was calling them. I spent hours standing on my mother's

14th-floor balcony looking down at people on the ground, trying to make them look up at me. It did work, occasionally. I also created a radionics device out of a shoebox, a tin can, some potentiometers—radio tuners—and some wires I picked up from RadioShack. You could put a picture of someone in the can and tune in to their frequency to send them good health or other benefits. This was a whole new world to explore, and I was excited to explore it.

The day came for me to return to the hospital to receive the results of the HIV test. I met with the same doctor who ordered both the open biopsy and the HIV test. Fortunately for me, the HIV test was negative. "Wahoo!" I thought. However, before I could wipe the sweat off my brow and celebrate, the doctor had further news. Since it wasn't HIV that was wiping out my kidneys, it was some other type of autoimmune attack. He was unsure exactly what the cause was, but the effect was I had very little kidney function remaining: end stage renal failure, he called it—my kidneys were failing.

Talk about a downer! "Kidney failure; what does that really mean?" I pondered. My mind wandered back to work, to the guy who sat in the cubicle beside me, Morgan Craig; he had kidney disease. The poor fellow. Quite often I would peak around the separating wall to see him sleeping on his desk. He looked tired and exhausted most of the time, he was very thin, and his skin color had a slight graying to it. "Is this where I'm heading? There must be some mistake," I thought. No mistake. The doctor was making a referral for me to see a nephrologist, Dr. Stephen Chow, who had an office on Coxwell Avenue, and told me he would be able to answer more of my questions.

Out of the pan and into the fire! This whole thing wasn't going to get better anytime soon. Strangely enough, I wasn't all that worried about it. Perhaps that little bit of meditation I had already done had shifted something in me. Normally, I'd be freaked out and worried every second of the day about what was next, but this time I didn't go there. In the material I was reading, there was stuff about healing and miracles that happened all the time. I needed to know more about that. That was the ticket out of this mess. I had chewed through the best portion of my mother's books; I needed a new source. On the way home, we stopped at a New Age bookstore that offered psychic readings in the office above.

Inside the bookstore, we were greeted by a fortysomething, eccentric-looking woman, whom I surmised was the psychic herself. She asked if I needed some help. I responded that, "I'm just getting into this stuff and I can't seem to get enough of it."

In response, she told me, as she attended to a bookshelf and without facing me, "It doesn't really mean much, unless you can apply it to your daily life."

"Talk about taking the wind out of my sails," I thought to myself. "Here I thought I was rolling right along on a path to be highly spiritual in no time, and now I hear I have to apply it to my life...And how does one do that anyhow?"

Next thing I knew, the woman startlingly half-jumped to face me, and cried out, "Did you feel that?"

Since she caught me off guard, I immediately froze. As I did, I felt a warm tingling sensation—a shiver—run down my spine, then answered "feel what?" as if I hadn't felt anything.

"Fear!" she replied, pausing briefly and walking away.

"Whoa! What was that all about?" I couldn't help but think she was talking about me. I replayed the last few moments repeatedly, in my mind, trying to figure out whether the warm tingling sensation I felt happened before she cried out, or in response to her crying out. If it had happened before, perhaps she was picking up on something in me. She was psychic, after all. If it was me, what was I supposed to be fearful about? In retrospect, I guess there was a lot I had to be fearful about...Just not at that moment. I had to admit, I was beginning to have those warm tingles from time to time. I never saw them as something negative, as they usually occurred when something special was happening; but in this case, they came as a response to a fright. Maybe it wasn't the same tingles? This is all too new to me. A puzzling encounter, to say the least. To this day, I have not been able to figure that one out.

I stayed with my mother for another two weeks, walking daily, back and forth, to the local shopping mall. I realized I could cut through the buildings across the street, to a path that traveled parallel to the street, directly to the mall. As I walked on that path, I had time to reflect about my life, as well as notice the people around me. It's as though I never really noticed them before. Yes, I noticed that there were always people: doing things, living their lives all around me, but I never really *took notice* of them. It's like time was slowing down, almost standing still now and then. I was beginning to notice the joy on the faces of parents as they played with their children in the park. I saw the pride on the face of the man selling fruit from the back of his truck (albeit illegally), and the pleasure his customers received, knowing they were buying fresh fruit from an authentic source. There was also screams of laughter from children as they swung high on the swing sets and slid joyfully down the slide. This was all there before; why didn't I notice? I was noticing now!

Once I got my staples removed, and my incision was starting to heal with all the walking, I was given the green light to drive again. There was a jazz festival taking place down on Queen Street. My two older sisters, Donna Johnson-Huggins and Paula Johnson, were going and invited me to join them. Donna lived on Jarvis Street at the time, so I drove over there, met them, and we began walking down Jarvis Street. As we approached Carlton Street going south, we hustled across to catch the tail end of the green light. Approaching the other side of the street, there were people pausing before crossing east to west across Jarvis Street. Just then, a woman who was waiting to cross Jarvis Street turned around, handed me a pamphlet. "Here, take this!" she said before crossing the street with the rest of the pedestrians. At the time, I didn't think anything of it until I looked down at the pamphlet and saw that it was about a spiritual event taking place in Toronto. Coincidence?

When we got down to the jazz festival celebrations, it was pandemonium! People were everywhere enjoying themselves with friends and family. That was the first time since my surgery I had walked such a long distance, and it was taking its toll. We decided to stop at a small bistro to rest and grab a bite to eat. The table we were sitting at was right at the front of the building, and the windows were open; we were face-to-face with the passersby.

Just then a young man ran up to the window, looked at me excitedly and said, "We're having an event at my church this evening. You should come!" I thought this was odd, because, let me clarify: I was sitting there with my two sisters, the three of us at a table waiting to eat, and this man approached and spoke only to me, as if they were not even there. "Hang on a second!" he continued, and then ran off and returned a few moments later with a flyer for his event. I smiled, and nodded in appreciation, and off he went. I wasn't sure what was going on, but stuff like that began happening all the time. Flyers, events, books, psychics, everything spiritual was coming my way, and in like fashion, I was taking it all in—couldn't get enough of it! My life was changing.

It was getting close to the time for me to return home, back to Peterborough, back to my life as I'd left it. After everything that happened over the past month, and everything I was now learning about life, how was I going to cope? Could I simply go back to the way things were? I lay on the bed, in my mother's guest room, contemplating how my life *used to be*. I focused in on what was happening just before I left, and I could see it all like in a dream...I was the observer, *watching myself*...The way I was...The way things used to be...

4

RUN DMC AND HEAVY D

You're under no obligation to be the same person
you were 5 minutes ago.

~ Alan Watts

"Your creatinine is 1,900! Get yourself some help!"
I sat dumbfounded—or was it depressed—across
from Dr. F. Coleman, the transplant nephrologist I
was referred to by Dr. Chow. Maybe it was because I was a little
pissy, or maybe it was because the good doctor didn't like the
fact that I wanted to heal my kidneys naturally, but I found this
guy to be a bit of an arrogant ass. By "Get yourself some help,"
he meant that I should start getting dialysis treatments to deal
with the toxins that were now building up, heavily, within my
body. Normal creatinine should be about 150 μmol per liter,
and mine was 1,900 μmol per liter (a little excessive wouldn't
you say?). I was starting to feel the effects of the toxicity in my
body. Creatinine is a waste product of muscle metabolism and is
usually filtered out of the blood by the kidneys and then passed
out of the body in urine. Since my kidneys were failing, I had
excess creatinine floating around my system twenty-four seven! I
constantly felt lethargic and nauseous. I had a bad metallic taste

in my mouth all the time and an overall sick feeling throughout my body. He was right; I just didn't want to admit it.

I got ratcheted-up to Dr. Coleman after multiple trips from Peterborough, back to Toronto, to see Dr. Chow for follow-up checkups. His solution was to manage the high blood pressure with hypertension meds and then load-up on prednisone to see if that would restore kidney function. That's when I was first introduced to *prednisone*; one of my favorites—NOT! It's a corticosteroid with immunosuppressive properties. When patients with my type of renal failure (which was finally diagnosed as FSG, focal-segmental glomerulonephritis) are given prednisone in large doses, it's supposed to slow the immune system from hammering on the kidneys and relieve the inflammation so the kidneys can function normally—in theory! It is a nasty drug, with plenty of side effects. The one I hated most, though, was when it puffed up my face, so I looked like a chipmunk with nuts in my cheeks. Not a very attractive look, and one that screamed, "I'm sick, and on drugs!"

When I thought about the final diagnosis of FSG, I wondered what started it all. To me it was explained like this: I had a bad virus or infection at some point, I might even have been treated for it and thought it was gone, but it managed to find a place to hide—in the fine workings of my kidneys, the glomeruli, where wastes and water are filtered from the blood. My immune system, in finding the virus hidden among the fine glomeruli, had difficulty distinguishing between the virus and the glomeruli cells. So it killed them both, in the process of trying to rid the body of the invader. I tried to think of a time when I had been really sick with a cold or the flu, but there were too many occasions to consider. Since I was a child, almost every other cold I got turned into bronchitis or pneumonia. In trying to narrow down the timeframe, I recalled having severe pain in my lower back when I would sit in the car on long drives. That seemed to happen in my university days and shortly thereafter. "Could it have been going on that long?" I wondered. They say the disease can remain chronic in the body for many years, with next to no signs, just waiting for the last grain of sand to topple the pillar. I had just come back from a trip to the Dominican Republic where I was sick as a dog for an entire day, throwing up and having the chills the whole time. Maybe it was that virus? Who knew? And what did it matter, really? It was here now, and I had to deal with it.

Being back in Peterborough was a real challenge. My life was no longer the same. The whole paradigm of my reality had shifted, and I wasn't sure how my old life fit into what I was learning spiritually. My job was the biggest challenge. As a tax auditor, I was required to *cold call* taxpayers to set up appointments to review their books and records. As you can imagine, people were not pleased to hear who was on the other end of the telephone. It was the proverbial *taxman* calling! While the job was a necessary evil, it nevertheless made you feel like you were the bad guy doing something everybody hated. Now that my heart and mind were both beginning to expand, I had a hard time constantly being the bearer of bad news. Perfect strangers hated you before they even got to know you. Talk about bad energy, swirling around you and pointed in your direction every day. At least, I still had the union stuff; there, at least I felt like I was helping people. As a result, I adjusted my daily schedules to focus more on my union duties, while doing the bare minimum tax auditing duties—just enough to have acceptable stats. Oh, the games we play!

My cubicle neighbor, Morgan Craig, and I were now a real pair. I was beginning to understand him a lot more; why he was so tired and lethargic all the time. After my appointment with Dr. Coleman, I made another revelation about Morgan. Dr. Coleman talked about the different types of dialysis: *peritoneal* and *hemodialysis*. In hemodialysis, you are hooked up to a machine that filters your blood: one line out of your body that transfers the *dirty* blood into the machine which cleans it, and one line in, that brings the *clean*, filtered blood back into your body. In peritoneal dialysis, bags of fluid (called dialysate) are run through a catheter into your stomach where the fluid remains for a few hours. During that time, the peritoneal membrane of your stomach acts as a filter and allows the wastes in your blood, and extra fluid, to pass into the dialysate. At the end of the waiting time, you release the dialysate, extra body fluid, and waste, into another bag, or into the toilet to be flushed away. That's when it clicked about Morgan. A couple of times I had gone into the bathroom when he was in there. Although he was behind the stall enclosure, I could hear him peeing for many minutes at a time—almost the whole time I was in the bathroom: did my thing, washed my hands and left...still going! I quite often wondered about that, but now I knew what was really going on. He was doing peritoneal dialysis throughout the day, while at work—what a warrior—and the peeing sound was really him emptying the dialysate from his stomach catheter into the toilet. "Wow, what a trip!" I couldn't imagine...Well...I could...now. Unwittingly, Morgan helped me to make up my mind about which type of dialysis I wanted to do when the time came—not that one! Fortunately, Dr. Coleman told me that, because of my size and build, peritoneal dialysis would probably not be an option. Thank my lucky stars!

At least there was one bright side to being back, I was able to pick up where I left off with Lorie. Funny how we met—and talk about manifesting your own destiny—I had just gotten out of a bad relationship about a year before, and at 32, while you're not over the hill, it's not the easiest thing to meet new people. You're too old for the bar crowd, and since I wasn't into the church group thing, or picking up women at the grocery store, there weren't too many options left. Anyhow, I was tired of the bar scene, and wasn't interested in anyone from that realm. From experience, people there were all caught up in outward appearances—the makeup and the muscle—and those relationships didn't tend to last much longer than the next morning, if you know what I mean. I was looking for somebody I could have a conversation with. I was trying to change. A couple of times in the bar, I would find a nice girl to talk to, only to see her walking out, tipsy, at the end of the night, hand-in-hand with one of the regular sharks. I could hardly blame her, or him for that matter, having seen a lot of myself in that same situation. Except now, the shoe was on the other foot. I was renting the basement space of a co-worker, Lysa Borland. I couldn't help but notice a picture she had on her home-office desk, as I walked by daily. When I asked her about it, she told me it was her brother and his wife, Lorie, on their wedding day. I quite often looked at that girl in the picture, and said to myself, "Why can't I meet a girl like that?" Something about her face was kind and compassionate—almost angelic—and although I didn't know her, she seemed to be very down-to-earth. Of course, there were the obvious requirements, for me at least, that she was pretty and looked like she took care of her body. Well as fate would have it, Lorie started to show up at Lysa's place for girls' night out. Through conversation with Lysa, I found out that Lysa's brother had split up with Lorie around Christmas. The whole separation thing came as a surprise—Lorie hadn't seen it coming. As a result, part of the girls' night out soirées was to buoy Lorie's spirits and help her get back into the swing of things. I met her once or twice at the house, as the girls would gather there before going out. Shortly after, I asked her out.

We hit it off and began to spend every spare moment together. Bless her heart, Lorie did not look upon my health challenges as a physical or emotional detraction from our new relationship. She was supportive and helped in any way that she could, with my newfound troubles. This was a huge benefit, as things were about to get REAL!

Real it was, as I sat in my dialysis chair for the first time. Dr. Coleman got me hooked up—literally—with dialysis in Oshawa, about a 45-minute drive from Peterborough. "No room at the Inn," was the word I got from the local DMC (Dialysis Management Clinics) which was the only shop in town; the Peterborough hospital did not yet have dialysis clinics. I looked up and gazed around the room. The pain and suffering I saw was almost unbearable. Some patients had walked in, as I had, but some were wheeled in on stretchers from the adjoining hospital. Expressions of anger, despair, denial, and fear were all around me…But there was acceptance too, on the faces of some who had come to grips with their new fate. "What am I doing here?" I thought. "I don't belong here. These cannot be my new peers in life. They can't be! I'm the guy. You know? The man! Not this. Noooo!" I was the one in denial, or shock for that matter. How did I end up here?

To me, dialysis was a cruel beast. Sure, I got the concept that it was a life-saving technology that could effectively keep me alive when my kidneys had gone down in flames in end-stage renal failure; but it had an uncanny way of creeping, unwantedly, into my daily life. First, was the fact that I had to have it three times a week and sit in a chair for three hours at a time—which seemed like forever! Secondly, on the first run, I had to have a neck catheter inserted into my right jugular vein: this is kind of like a big intravenous line that travels down inside your body toward your heart, and had two lumens—a line in, and a line out—and each of these lines had a red or a blue twist-off access lid. This is where the nurses connected you to the dialysis machine. All good...For dialysis...But was a huge eyesore as it remained connected to you twenty-four seven; you had to wear it around town, every day, even when not having dialysis. Not to mention, while they put some lidocaine on your skin before, virtually, ramming it in, it still hurt like hell! Of course, once I was hooked up and going, it wasn't so bad...Except for feeling sorry for myself. I had to get used to this new way of living.

Before long, an opening became available at the DMC in Peterborough; I grabbed it up! This is where most of my dialysis life took place, and where I came to experience all the joys of the process (cue sarcasm). This was also where I got my first taste of rotating doctors and nurses. Just when you thought you were getting used to one doctor, you got exposed to another—along with the concomitant need for each to do things in his or her own way or change protocols as they saw fit. Somewhere along the line-up, it was deemed that my neck catheter did not allow sufficient blood flow through the dialysis machine, enough to clean my six-foot-three frame, effectively. I moved from the neck catheter, to a chest catheter, and finally to a fistula—an abnormal connection between two blood vessels. In a separate procedure for my forearm fistula, a surgeon disconnected a vein (from the top of my wrist, which returned blood from my hand) and reconnected it to my artery (near the underside of my wrist)—all hidden below the surface, under the skin—creating a loop through which blood was pumped directly from my heart, down my arm, and back up again. As the blood flowed strongly through this loop, to touch the fistula you could feel a vibration, like a little engine was purring underneath, which was called *the thrill*. The only problem was the fistula didn't have those wonderful little red and blue caps to connect to. Each time you arrived for your dialysis treatment; the nurses were required to *cannulate* the fistula. To cannulate, the nurses used a large needle, about the size of the tube inside a pen, which they inserted into the engorged fistula vein to draw blood into the dialysis machine. A second needle was inserted above the first, a few inches away, in order to return the blood into the body. The fistula allowed for the hemodialysis to clean the toxins from my blood, as well as two days' worth of fluid buildup. This process was more complete, but also much more painful. Quite often, as the nurses jammed those big needles into your fistula vein, they pushed in a little too deep. "Ouch, you've gone too deep!" I'd admonish.

"No, look," the nurse would respond as she flagged the needle back to show that blood was flowing. "It's not too deep. I know what I'm doing!" All I could do was to roll my eyes and shake my head, knowing that once I got home after the treatment, the black and blue bruising would begin to encircle the area that was dug too deep.

"Oh, the battle scars one has to endure," and bite your tongue, because you're lucky to be able to receive such treatments…And kids are starving in Africa…

The fistula was, in fact, better than the chest catheter, and if not for any other reason, it couldn't get contaminated as easily as the chest catheter—or *permacath*, as it was also called. My mind ran back to a time when my chest catheter got infected. At first, I didn't know it had become contaminated, and went back and forth from my dialysis treatments *stirring the pot,* so to speak. The chest catheter was much like the neck catheter, except that it was inserted in the middle of the right chest, upwards, so it could meet one of the large veins that emptied directly into the heart. Once contaminated, it would pump the infection throughout your entire body. I wondered why I would feel good for a day, then crappy after my dialysis treatment. Okay, crappy is an understatement. One night, during the infection period, I could barely eat my dinner. I went upstairs to bury my face in the pillow to *scream* as loudly as I could, "AAAAAH! WHAT THE FUCK IS GOING ON! WHY ARE YOU TORTURING ME LIKE THIS! AAAAAH!" The infection had taken over my body so powerfully, it felt like I was being electrocuted, unendingly. The fiasco ended up in a trip to the ER—in Oshawa—to have two large bottles of antibiotics pumped through my system. You live, and you learn!

Even though I was now being indoctrinated into the dialysis world, I was still highly focused on using natural means to heal my kidney. Most of my nephrologists thought I was nuts, because they were so certain that the kidneys could not repair themselves, no matter what holistic, or allopathic (medical), protocol was used. One of Lorie's cousins was working with a reputable Naturopathic Doctor, Mikhael Adams, so I found myself regularly travelling from Peterborough, to Coburg, to see him. Before I got my forearm fistula, the doctors were planning a surgery to remove a vein in my leg to use in my forearm fistula; they didn't feel that the veins in my forearm were big enough for sufficient flow. The first time I spoke with Dr. Adams about my condition, and whether his methods could heal my kidney, he said that they could. That's all the assurance I needed to cancel that surgery. I felt it was a message from above, to save me from the grief of that procedure. Through Dr. Adams, I was taking several tinctures and tiny, globule pills to balance my body, push out any infection in the kidneys, and repair the damage within them. This went on for many months (and at significant cost), and while I felt better overall, I still needed weekly dialysis to do the job my kidneys weren't. In my final visit with Dr. Adams, he seemed perplexed as to why my kidneys had not recovered. He always used a strange technique: he waved a small reflective wand—that looked like a leather key fob—over my wrist, while he took my pulse with his other hand. This is how he queried the body as to what was wrong, what was missing, and what was needed to fix it. "Your body tells me that it is in balance," he offered. "Your kidneys should have gotten better by now. There is nothing more I can do. It looks like the rest is up to you." He was somehow implying that I was not mentally, or emotionally, prepared for a healing, and that the balance of work to allow this miracle to occur, was on me.

"The rest is up to me?" This statement played over, and over, and over, in my mind, like a broken record. "What haven't I done? What am I doing wrong? What do I need to do?" I felt that it was unfair to have this yoke laid on me in this way. In this new, magical world of holistic health, I believed this doctor should've had those answers for me: some advice, or some direction as to how I was supposed to make that happen. He was a doctor of herbs and tinctures; maybe what I needed was something more energetic. I continued searching for something more spiritual, or metaphysical, in nature. If it exists, I'll find it.

5

EN-LARGER THAN LIFE

When the student is ready, the teacher will appear.

~ Confucian proverb

"Hello?" I answered.

"Is this Kirk?" the other voice asked.

"Yes, it's him," I replied.

"Kirk, it's Dr. Whatley. I just got the results back from your chest X-ray and I just had to call you right away. Has anyone ever told you your heart was enlarged?"

"No," I countered, remembering Dr. Whatley had never called me at home before, and now that he had, his voice had the tone of the two a.m. police officer, bringing bad news to the parents of an accident victim.

"Well, it's enlarged now, in fact, quite enlarged. You need to go see a heart specialist right away..."

"What the fuck!" I thought to myself. "What now?" I had been feeling a little bit under the weather, and was presenting with, what seemed like, just a regular cold. Unfortunately, with me, there were no regular colds; they always seemed to get down into my chest and I'd end up coughing like a bass drum, and hacking up brightly colored sputum, repeatedly. Although I was getting dialysis regularly, I was not my typical self—more of a weakened version that seemed to get sick much more often. This time, it seemed like the cold was lasting a little too long for my liking, and the thoughts of it turning into pneumonia was a little too painful to bear, so I'd made an appointment to go see my GP, Dr. Richard Whatley. After listening to my lungs, he sent me to the lab to get a chest X-ray; that's what precipitated the call.

Within a week, I was referred to a heart specialist in Peterborough, Dr. Robert Howes. I had, foolishly, mentioned to Dr. Whatley that I was trying to heal my kidneys naturally. Consequently, the word was getting around that I wasn't taking my plight seriously, was anti-medicine, and refused drugs. Dr. Howes thought it necessary to use scare tactics to get me to comply. He laid out a plan for more tests, and more drugs, announcing: "If you do not help yourself, you will die!" He bellowed this statement out, with his office door open to the fully packed waiting room nearby. I could feel my ire beginning to rise—no, not rise—boil! I was pissed!

"What a jackass!" I thought to myself. "Typical, small-town Peterborough." With this heart problem, on top of my already-problematic kidney situation, I needed to think bigger, smarter. I needed to go to Toronto! With my ire up, I brazenly asked Dr. Howes for a second opinion; a referral to a cardiologist in Toronto. He complied, and I was referred to Dr. Gary Newton at Mount Sinai Hospital in Toronto.

My first meeting with Dr. Newton was pleasant. He was a mild-mannered soul whose mannerisms and knowledge gave me the impression that he knew what he was talking about. Of course, now having my cardiologist out of town, I had to pile on an extra hour-and-a-half drive from Peterborough to Toronto in order to see him, but to me it was worth it. Not that there weren't more drugs to take, but his delivery of my new predicament, and what was needed to resolve it on a temporary basis, was somehow more palatable to me. "Why temporary?" I wondered. Temporary, because a new consideration was on the table—the possibility of a *heart transplant*! He explained that a normal heart should be like a closed fist, solid and strong, but mine was now enlarged, flabby, and weak. It was no longer strong enough to push the blood through my body efficiently, nor effectively; cardiomyopathy, he called it. "Whoa! That's messed up," I thought. "So now, on top of a kidney transplant—to get away from the dialysis nightmare—I might need a heart transplant as well? What…is…going… on?"

The burden of this new revelation, along with dialysis, end-stage renal failure, neck and chest catheters, fistulas, the list goes on and on…was getting to be too much. Add in the self-defeating failure to heal myself—or balance my body so that it could heal itself— and it would have been very easy to just lay down and die. But that wasn't me: the new me that emerged from the realization that I had to welcome more spirituality into my life. I understood that one's life can be represented by a triangle, and on each side of the triangle is an element of one's life. On one side you have your physical attributes, on another mental or academic attributes, and on the last side soulful or spiritual attributes; all these attributes needed to be in balance. Prior to the walk-in clinic, my life was only focused on the physical and the mental sides of the triangle. Without the spiritual side, the triangle could collapse, and that's essentially what was happening now. Still, something inside was telling me that if I worked hard to catch up with the spiritual side of myself, such that it was as strong as the other two sides, I could get on top of all of these problems happening in my life. This was a battle between me and me. But I was a stubborn S.O.B. Just tell me I can't do something, and I'll do anything in my power to prove you wrong. I was feeling that I'd failed myself and I couldn't let that happen. Now I had to prove *myself* wrong.

The search was on for books, or any kind of material, that would support me in this task. While sitting in my dialysis chair for three hours at a time, I could simply watch TV and waste that time, or use that time wisely to learn ways to help balance my spiritual self. One afternoon, I made my way over to the *Inner Circle* bookstore to look for a book called the *Tibetan Book of*

Living and Dying. I, inwardly, felt a draw to Eastern spirituality teachings, sensing that spirituality and religion were two separate creatures. Spirituality should be the foundation of religion, but from what I could see in history, as well as present day, that religion had taken on a life of its own. It seemed some religions were becoming bereft of spirituality in their dogmatic teachings. Religion cannot stand alone without spirituality, but spirituality can stand alone without religion. Why was I choosing this book? I'd heard many people talk about it, and besides that, the issue of *death,* and my understanding of it, was now of constant concern; I might as well dig in and get to know it a little better.

The Inner Circle bookstore was an eclectic collection of personal growth, self-help, spirituality, and metaphysical books and paraphernalia. The people working there were very grassroots-granola friendly, like beatniks and hippies right out of Woodstock. The store offered various metaphysical teachings in the back, and an incense-scented bookstore in the front. As I perused the shelves, there were so many titles to choose from. Walking the aisles, searching for the book I came to buy, I noticed a book with a long, black-haired woman in an orange gown on the front cover, staring at me. The book was entitled *Autobiography of a Yogi,* and I took it down from the shelf to see who this woman was. As it turned out, it wasn't a woman at all, but a somewhat feminine looking man whose gaze had connected with me in some strange way. I skimmed the book to surmise that this man, Paramahansa Yogananda, was born an *avatar*—a God realized soul who had reincarnated back on earth in order to bring spiritual teachings to those left behind. The purpose of his book was to tell of his struggles, and successes, in living as a human man, while still strongly connected to God and the etheric realms. I found the concept interesting, but then realized I came for a different book, so I moved along to find that publication. In short order, I found the *Tibetan Book of Living and Dying*, and purchased it. After I drove home, I opened the bag to retrieve my new book and have a look at it. To my surprise, it wasn't the book I had set out to get, but in my hand, staring at me, was *Autobiography of a Yogi.* "What the...?" I would later come to understand that it was all in Divine order.

Books were one way of opening up to spirituality, but I felt like I needed some hands-on work, as well. I had heard of a healing modality called *reiki* and, from some of my own research, understood that it was a means of channeling higher levels of energy to damaged parts of the body, to allow them to heal more rapidly. I also read that it was something one could not obtain just by reading; a channel had to be opened up in you by a Reiki Master. That Master could attune you to Level I for personal use, or Level II to work on others as a practitioner or therapist. I searched the newspapers and the Yellow Pages for anyone offering Level I reiki classes and was repeatedly drawn back to a teacher named Bernard Morin.

"Ahhhhhhhhhhhh..." That was the long, drawn-out sound they asked me to make as I lay on a massage table and two strangers lightly laid their hands on me and *supposedly* channeled healing energy to me. I felt kind of silly, but at this point I was willing to try anything to get my heart and kidneys working properly again. Bernie, the Reiki Master, walked around from table to table overseeing the others who were on tables receiving a treatment much like myself. It was the last day of this four-day event and we had already received the teachings and our attunements to the *Universal Life Force Energy* of reiki. Then something happened. Something I didn't expect. To my surprise, the Ahhhh...turned to Wahhhh...as I unearthed an ancient burial ground of emotion and began sobbing uncontrollably. Memories and feelings, I had thought long forgotten, were resurfacing for me to review. I heard the practitioner's voice softly say, "You're in a safe place now. It's okay to look at what happened back then and feel what you couldn't before—because it wasn't safe. Just let it go." And I did. Boy, did I ever! They gave me just the permission I needed to unleash those pent-up emotions. The relief I felt after the workshop was indescribable. I will always remember that experience; it was an awakening!

What were these emotions and memories I was dredging up? I couldn't recall all of them, but two issues stuck out in my mind—*my father,* and *women.* My father was a strict man with one parenting credo: his way or the highway! When I was young, I was a bit of a badass, getting into trouble from time to time. He was so caught up in amassing his fortune, he forgot to buy us toys to play with. One evening, when I was eight years old, my family was shopping at *Woolco* department store, I slipped away from the rest and headed to the toy section. There, I filled my pockets with matchbox cars, toys, and other small items. Of course, on the way out we got stopped, and I had to give the stuff back. My father was incensed...or *embarrassed* that we had to be taken to a back security room and searched like common criminals. When we got home, he made me stand on the first landing of the staircase to the upper level. There, he took off his belt and beat me, repeatedly, while my mother and my three sisters watched. They all sobbed fearfully, as he continued, lash after lash. My mother later described to me that it looked like he was *getting off* and demanded that he stop. The badass part of the story was that, while he was beating me, I cried buckets full of tears, yet what worried me most was not that the beating wouldn't stop, it was the thought of what would happen if the stolen magnifying glass I held back, stashed in my sock, would have fallen out onto the floor. True gangsta! That was just one of the many times I received beatings from my father. My parents split up when I was thirteen and a part of me was glad he was gone. The reiki experience revealed that I still struggled to forgive him.

The second issue was women...or was it love? I wasn't sure, but let's look at it from the issue of women. From the time I was in junior high, and then onto high school, I was good at athletics. In almost any sport—football, basketball, soccer, track and field, badminton, archery, you name it—I excelled! Being good at sports naturally drew the attention of the opposite sex. Human nature at its best; I became popular with the girls. Also, given that my parents had split up and my sisters and I were now living in low-income housing with my mother, I began to mix with a lot of kids that no longer went to school. In this environment, getting with girls was one of the favorite pastimes. Coincidentally, because I was six-foot-three at fifteen and able to grow a moustache, I could get into the liquor store, beer store and many of the clubs in my hometown of Kitchener. Even though I was still a kid at that time, I got together with women in their early 20s and beyond. However, the issue wasn't so much how I came to be with the ladies, but why. The answer to that was *love*. This revelation was only coming to me now. The reiki had woken this up somehow. Who knows? It helped me to understand why, when I met a great girl and she wanted to get together again (or maybe even begin a relationship), initially I'd say yes. Then as soon as one of my buddies called me up, and said "Hey, let's go out…" I'd cancel that follow-up engagement to go search for another *victim*.

Some may say, "That's what all guys do. They think with their dicks!" That didn't resonate with me, though. Was the sex so important? Not really, because as soon as it was over, you just wanted to leave. Then why? I realized, *I just wanted to be loved!* Foolishly, I thought sex was love, and I wanted to experience as many different types of love as possible. Why was I so bereft of love? My mother loved me, my sisters loved me, my friends loved me, even my dad loved me (though he had never verbalized it) in his own way. So what was this deep desire to be loved? In time, I would come to understand it, but for now it only seemed to haunt me. All these relationships—many, one-nighters—made me wonder who I had hurt. I'd decided, a while ago, that I'd done this enough and vowed to be loyal to one woman—Lorie. I was putting my foot down on this issue and was determined not to fail!

My Reiki Master, Bernie, also taught classes on shamanic journeying and healing. Another modality I was drawn to. In a class of about eight people, we were taught how to use steady drumming beats to connect to spirit-guide animals called *totems,* in a realm called *non-ordinary space.* This was a two-day event, and I can recall, after driving home from the workshop on the first day, seeing a fox race ahead of me as I drove. A small, grey fox was sprinting up the gravel shoulder, kicking up dust as it sped along ahead of me. Then it was gone, like the apparition you weren't meant to see. After that, I saw foxes everywhere. They were speaking to me in that unheard, unseen language called *shamanism*. After all, the fox was my totem and had been for many years. I just didn't know it. I found that out through a shamanic journey I had taken in the class. In shamanic journeying, you enter a dreamlike state while you are awake, and can interact with nature and animals that guide you in life—if you're willing to look for them. At first when I journeyed, a part of me thought, "this is just my imagination playing tricks on me." Later, when other animals brought messages to me, or when things that I saw while journeying began to ring true in my life, I could no longer deny their authenticity. I began to rely on these messages to guide me in my life, moving forward.

My life was definitely changing. Everything about it was different. I had taken long-term disability (LTD) from work, under the advice from my manager. Oh, and that corporate auditor job that I was competing for? I was successful, and placed second on the list! I had passed my CGA exam, which in turn validated my requirements for the position, and was waiting to be called. I did my best to stay at the job, after returning from the walk-in clinic *awakening* in Toronto, so I could bump up from the proprietorship auditor that I was, to the corporate auditor position I had competed for, but I just couldn't hang in there. I felt sickly and toxic every day, and even though it would've been worth the pay raise, I could no longer pretend to be working when I no longer had it in me—just for the money. My manager convinced me there was no shame in taking LTD. "You paid for it. You might as well use it!" he suggested. Right, he was. I left there and never looked back. As my new spiritual side was building, I could no longer tolerate the negative undertones associated with being *the taxman*—ever hated, always denigrated.

Changes were happening on the home front, too. Lorie and I were inseparable. We had moved in together, and as fate would have it, we were blessed with a gift: Lorie was pregnant! This came as somewhat of a surprise since she and her previous husband could not conceive. They were both tested, but egotistically, he decried that the problem was on her side; she thought she was infertile. As it turned out, she was not. A baby was on the way! We were not yet married, and neither of us savored the idea of having a child out of wedlock, so we made a plan... and executed it. Since she had been married before, and I was not at my best, we decided to drive to Niagara Falls and get married; we eloped! On July 18, 1998 we were married in Niagara Falls, New York, and Lorie Masterson became Lorie Johnson for the first time. All was good on the home front.

Nathaniel James Johnson was born on April 13, 1999. A happy, little bundle of joy. When he was young, he looked unmistakably like his mother; comparing his baby picture to Lorie's baby picture, they were almost identical. "Whatever happened to them Johnson genes?" I chuckled. "Maybe later!" We shared our newfound joy with my first son, Travis. Given my weakened state, Lorie graciously took up the mantle of the long drives to pick him up from Kitchener for visits. Even Travis's mother, Laurie Moxey (nee Smallwood), chipped in and met her halfway. I was grateful to both women, who took on some of my burdens to help me continue a relationship with my son. That was uber-important to me!

As a father of two sons, a husband, a son, a brother, a friend to many, and a man whose health had just come crashing down with no end in sight, I endlessly contemplated why this was happening to me, and how it all may end—soon. While I was reading about, and researching, death, I came across an organization called Hospice that offered teachings on how to deal with death. Hospice also gave insight into what the caregivers of end-of-life patients had to go through. This seemed like something I should learn and signed up for their courses. Classes were about topics surrounding grief and bereavement—what they were, and how to deal with them. Before long, I realized these classes were training for volunteers to be able to go into the homes of those who were near-death, to provide comfort to them, as well as their caregivers and families. "The perfect place to use my newfound reiki skills, and maybe there was the possibility the healing energy could help some of these poor souls get better," I mused. Wrong! The administrators didn't want anyone giving these folks *false hope*—as they called it. They felt reiki could be used to ease the pain of passing but did not want it to be used for anything else. Inside, I hoped that if I could use it for them, and be successful in healing them, that it could somehow work for me, too. Wishful thinking! In the end, the training was still very useful; not only for my own edification but also for events that were yet to come.

PART II

KARMIC DEBT

2000 - 2006

6

MOUNT SINAI'S COMMANDMENTS

If you do not change direction, you may end up where you are heading.

~ Buddhist proverb

"If I can't do it myself, the way I want, then here you go! Take my body and do whatever you want with it. Fix it!" That's the mantra that played over and over in my head at Mount Sinai Hospital in Toronto. With that attitude, I just lay in bed, in a conscious, comatose state, and just got sicker and sicker.

I was angry! I was angry and I needed someone to blame. It was a few days after Travis had come for one of his visits. I always enjoyed the time we spent together, and this was no different, except for the fact that he was sick as a dog. I watched as green snot ran down his nose and he snorted it up, again and again, like a yo-yo. Yes, as a parent, colds, flu, and sickness were all part of the game, but for me, in my present much-weakened state, these complications could be *deadly*. "Could his mother not have known that he was sick?" I thought. "Maybe she knew he was sick, but this was her weekend off and she was taking it, no matter what? Was there a chance that I wouldn't get sick?" No, none! And I did. One doozy of a sickness! At that point, I could barely walk ten meters without having to stop to catch my breath. My lungs were filling up and my heart was going down. I called Dr. Newton in Toronto and he told me to come right away.

After he took a look at me, he told me "Your heart is in pretty rough shape. Since you're here, you should admit yourself to the hospital." My heart sank like the Titanic. I did not see that coming...

I was feeling sorry for myself. The words of Dr. Mikhail Adams played again in my head, "The rest is up to you." I had failed myself somehow. Having tried homeopathic globules and tinctures, as well as the energetic healing techniques I had learned recently, I had done my best to resolve *the rest is up to you* threat, to no avail. Delving into the holistic healing world, researching and studying various techniques, I couldn't help but notice that where holistic health was making a dent in the healthcare industry, it was soon shot down or debunked as quackery. There was a war going on between allopathic and holistic (or alternative) medicine. I saw myself on the alternative side of that war. Now I was in the hands of the enemy, or so I thought at that time.

Room number one is where I resided, directly across from the nurses' station, in the CCU (Coronary Care Unit), on the 16th floor of Mount Sinai Hospital in Toronto. I had only been there for a few days but was already starting to see the routine. The staff doctor in charge would make his rounds with the newbies, the residents—or doctors in training—and stop off at each room to present the condition of each patient and discuss next steps. This was beginning to irritate me because, up until this point, no one had taken the time to help me understand what was wrong. Of course, I knew I was in end-stage renal failure, requiring dialysis, and that my heart was weak and enlarged, known as cardiomyopathy. But what caused it all? Okay, yes, I also knew that I now needed two transplants, a kidney and a heart, but I kept hearing the doctors saying "...Your particular condition..."

"What do you mean, *your* particular condition?" I pondered. "You people have done transplants before, haven't you? Why is this any different?" There were so many unanswered questions, and on this day I had simply had enough. I looked up from my hospital bed as the doctor was blathering out his diatribe to the minions about me, as if I wasn't there. It was too much. I broke down and started to sob, whilst beseeching the doctor to tell me what was going on with me. The group froze…And looked down upon me sympathetically, while still trying to embody that steely disposition of a professional-to-be.

But instead of explaining to me, the patient, what his thoughts were about my condition, in layman's terms, he simply indicated, "It looks like Mr. Johnson is having a bad day. Maybe we should leave him alone to rest and come back another time." Then they all walked out. If I was beginning to think that I was in bed with the enemy, this cemented it.

The word that I had been hospitalized was now getting around to my family. I can recall a conversation I had with my eldest sister, Donna, who came to visit. I was allowed out of my room for this visit, and she and I took the elevator down to the first floor and sat outside the front of the building—situated at the T-intersection of University Avenue and Gerrard Street. Donna had attended Bernie's shamanic workshop with me and shared my interest in metaphysics. I voiced some of my experiences with her and my search for answers. I was in a state of helpless confusion and was outwardly asking, "First the kidney stuff, and now a heart transplant? I keep asking myself why this is all happening to me? What did I do to deserve this?"

"Didn't you say that you wanted all of your karma now, all at once?" Donna questioned.

"Yes, I guess I did. I did ask for it to come all at once!" I replied (cue epiphany). In that moment, it was though a huge weight was lifted off my shoulders. I now recalled that I had previously spoken to Donna about *karma*—the universal law of cause and effect that we are all subject to—and that I no longer wanted to carry around the potentially damaging burdens of my past actions in this life, nor the many past lives before this one. "Bring it on!", I thought. In building up that spiritual side of my triangle, understanding, accepting, and getting rid of karma was a big part of that process. Through the book *Autobiography of a Yogi*, the Yogi-avatar Paramahansa Yogananda created an organization called Self-Realization Fellowship based in Los Angeles, California. The organization taught high-level yoga and meditation techniques, to open oneself to the truth behind the mysteries of life. It was through these lessons that I learned about karma, and the necessity to rid oneself of it in order to be truly free. Now it was all coming back to me. Amazing how, once one takes responsibility for their past actions, it begins to clear the slate of your life for new possibilities.

That was the day it dawned on me. The thought of all thoughts fell across my consciousness like sunrise over the ocean on a clear, cloudless day. "If I do not take part in my own healing in this hospital, I will die." Hospitals, and everyone in them, are great and necessary. But if you leave your life in their hands completely, while blindfolding yourself to what goes on, it's pure suicide, plain and simple. I came to realize that if I really wanted to check out, the universe had given me all the opportunity I needed to do so. All I had to do was give up!

Awakening from my conscious-trance state, I wanted to do everything for myself. Unfortunately, there is only so much they will allow you to do in a critical care ward of a major hospital, but I had to try. Anything I could do for myself, I did, and I soon began to take control of my life once again. I began to see the connection holistic medicine and allopathic (conventional) medicine have with each other. Conventional medicine patches you up and gives you the drugs to preserve your life. That precious preservation then gives holistic medicine the time to heal the root of your illness, and allows your body to, once again, become whole. With this new understanding, I used my medical incarceration to reflect on life, and I used my remaining time in the hospital to return to contemplation and meditation. The war was over...or so I thought.

I needed a heart transplant but had to wait until one became available. The plan was to keep me alive until then. So I was hooked up intravenously to a drug called *dobutamine*—24 hours a day, seven days a week. This drug was needed to keep my heart beating more forcefully. While plugged-in to the dobutamine, I was able to live a normal life, albeit from my single room on the 16th floor of a hospital.

Every couple of weeks, the CCU was managed by a different senior cardiologist of the hospital. I had no problem with that. In fact, who better to be in charge than the best the hospital had to offer. What I did have a problem with, was that every two weeks, the new managing doctor would try to wean me off of my life-sustaining drug—to see if my heart would operate well enough on its own, to send me home. I dreaded this practice because every time they performed the slow, controlled reduction, I gradually slumped over, shrivelled up, and returned to the weak, sickly state in which I originally entered the hospital. No matter how I complained, this practice continued. It seemed as though each successive doctor had not read the previous doctors' notes and performed the procedure as if they were the first to think of it. *Brilliant!*

At least I was getting some strength back. I was now able to get up and, with my dobutamine-drip-laden pole in hand, pace the halls to get some exercise. The CCU was set up in a U-shape, surrounding the nurse's station, so I was able to walk the full U-shape of the CCU, through a door, past the corridor with the elevators, and back to the start. Thinking back to my track and field days, that was *one lap of the track*. On one occasion, I came across a teenager, about 17, in a wheelchair, doing his best to drag himself along the corridor without help. I took an interest in this young fellow, and wheeled him, along with my own pole, for a distance. As I got to know him, he was struggling with his predicament. "How was it that a lad so young was in need of a heart transplant?" I wondered. I'm not sure if I ever did get the answer, but I certainly found out he had a short, nasty temper that he flashed on the nurses and staff of the CCU. Having my room across from the nurse's station, I quite often overheard the conversations surrounding this young man, and the problems they were having. Then, one day, he was gone! I asked the nurses where the young lad from the end of the hall had gone?

"He got his heart." She said, guiltily. I could tell from her demeanor, as well as overhearing the chatter in the hallway, that the nurses had hoped that I would get a heart first. I had been there first, so I should get served first—that type of thing. They also felt this young fellow's hostility should have, somehow, played a part in who was deserving of the next transplant. I can't say that being overlooked didn't mess around with my head…a little… wondering if I'd ever get my turn. Nevertheless, I couldn't bear him any ill will just because his number came up before mine. All he ever wanted to do was to go home and play with his dog. A few weeks had passed without hearing any news about the kid; not that it was any of my business. Then one day, I was speaking to one of the doctors (who I had a better-than-usual relationship with) and asked about him.

Almost whispering, to keep the message on the down-low, she told me the news. "He didn't make it. He got his transplant and had been discharged, then died in the backyard playing with his dog. He didn't suffer." I was stunned! Nothing is guaranteed. What stood out for me most, about the whole encounter with this kid, was the power of one's own thoughts and words. All he ever wanted was to go home and play with his dog. And go home he did…But not to his physical home on this earth, but to our Father's home in heaven. He got his wish. I reminded myself to pay attention to the messages I was putting out there. Words have power!

Even though I was making peace with my own situation, living in the hospital was still very uncomfortable. I couldn't sleep at night and found myself pacing the halls at all hours. The doctors tried all kinds of meds to help me to sleep: lorazepam, clonazepam, all the *pams,* and other sleep-inducing drugs. Nothing worked! My problem was ratcheted up into another category of drugs called the *antipsychotics.* "That didn't sound good," I thought. "After all, I wasn't cracked, was I?" One night as I lay in bed, I looked over to a chair in the corner of the room and could swear someone was sitting there, in the dark. The light from the Toronto skyline outside my window lit up the room, just enough to make things out. I could discern the dark shape of an entity sitting there, as though it were made of shadow. Next, I found myself feeling uncomfortable. The dobutamine line was taped to my arm, to keep it from pulling out of the intravenous insertion point, on the top of my right wrist. A feeling came over me—that I couldn't take it anymore! My skin was covered in the goop left behind by access lines being taped to me every day! I'd had enough and began to tear it off…and kept going, down to the intravenous line itself…Out it came. Next, horns and alarms were going off and the nurses burst into my room. They asked me what was going on. They seemed baffled as to why I would disconnect my lifeline, the dobutamine, the only thing keeping me alive. I did my best to assure them that I wasn't losing it; I wasn't going crazy. They got me reconnected and situated back in bed, turned the lights off, and closed the large sliding door to my room—leaving only a six-inch opening so they could peak in on me during the night.

There it was again…The dark being sitting in the chair. "Fuuuuuuck…" A chill ran down my spine. I'm not sure how, but next thing I knew, I found myself having dialogue with this specter. It was telling me to GET OUT! So once again, I peeled off my bandages. This time, however, having watched the nurses connect my dobutamine many times, I knew enough to silence the pump alarm, clamp off my intravenous insert, then kink the line and cap-off the dobutamine so it wouldn't leak on the floor. Then, I got out of bed and headed for the door. Just as I got to the door to walk out, I paused, "What am I doing? The way the nurses looked at me, they must have thought I was losing my mind. But I wasn't. I can't let them see that I had done this all over again. I had the presence of mind to unhook myself correctly. "What the fuck am I doing?" I asked myself. "Why am I listening to this fucking thing in the corner?" Then I got angry and shouted telepathically, "NO! I'm not getting out. YOU GET OUT!" The next second, I felt a wave of energy brush past me, through me, and out the six-inch opening of the door, like the rush of breeze you feel when the subway passes by. It was gone! I breathed a sigh of relief, returned to my bed, reconnected myself without alerting anyone, and went to sleep.

"What the heck was that all about?" I questioned the next morning as I thought about the night before. "Had I exorcised some type of demon that resided in me? What was that thing?" I guess I'll never know...because I don't think I'll be sharing that story with anyone, anytime soon. Speaking of demons, it was almost time for dialysis. Yes, I was still getting dialysis three times a week. The set-up guys would roll in a machine and hook it up to the plumbing in my room. Then, the nurse would show up shortly after that to pop the needles into my fistula and get the blood flowing. Every so often, a nephrologist would show up to check how things were going and to make sure they were taking enough fluid off during the treatments. Prior to entering the hospital, I had already figured out what my *dry weight* was. Dry weight is the number they used to enter into and the dialysis machine keypad to calculate how much fluid would be removed during the treatment. At this point in my renal failure, I no longer made urine. In other words, I didn't pee anymore. Every drink I had, the milk in my cereal, the liquid in my soup, etc., had to be accounted for. I was only allowed a thousand millilitres of fluid per day. Since I was dialyzed every other day, I should only have about two liters of fluid removed, along with the toxins. If I weighed 92.5 kg, and my dry weight was 90 kg, then I had 2.5 liters (one liter per kg) to remove during the treatment. However, since being in the hospital, my weight had dropped significantly. I was around 200 pounds when admitted, but was now reduced to a *buck seventy-five* pounds, or 79 kg dry weight. The nephrologists had this strange test that they would do. They would ask you to turn your head to the left to look at the side of your neck. Somehow, they could tell whether you had the correct dry weight or not. From experience, having now had dialysis for a couple of years, I knew my dry weight was correct. She, on the other hand, did not, and instructed the dialysis nurse to take off more fluid. "Okay... I hope you know what you're doing..." was all I could say.

Lorie would come to visit me at the hospital as often as possible. With me being a full-time resident in the hospital, she was now a single parent, back at home in Peterborough. The good thing was her parents lived close by, and they were more than happy to help, taking Nathan whenever they could. On one of her visits, we were busy catching up—her, with life at home, and me, with life in the hospital. As I listened to her, I noticed some strange, colorful, little toy-like visions appearing in front of my eyes; they were in front of me, yet not in the room. I tried to focus-in, to see exactly what they were, but they were constantly moving from the left of my vision to the right, making it difficult to focus on them. "What were these small apparitions?" I wondered. "Was it my spiritual eye awakening (wishful thinking)?" I just had to find out. I followed the anomaly from left...across the front...to the right...and so far to the right...that I found myself physically turning my head to the right...to catch up with the vision... as far as I could go...Until... Darkness!

Alarms were blaring, doctors and nurses were rushing into the room. The display on my monitor read 200 bpm! I was having a seizure. Every muscle in my body stiffened, my teeth clenched, and I shook inexhaustibly where I lay on the bed. I'm not sure how the medical crew got this to stop, but in a short while it subsided. My body felt the way it did after I had run my first 400-meter race. Being a 200-meter sprinter, I took off hard—not knowing that I had to save some kick for the turn, and the final 100—everything seized, my stride reduced, and I stumbled across the finish line before toppling over. Finished and in desperate need of recovery. Why had this seizure happened? The next day I was wheeled down to the Cath Lab for an angiogram, to check the status of my heart. I can still remember those evocative words, "This man is as dry as a bone!"

Notes were made in my chart, but I made a point of asking the doctor to tell the nephrologist what caused the seizure, and that my dry weight should be adjusted accordingly. He agreed and suggested that it should be adjusted by at least a couple of kilos. Next time I saw the nephrologist, she said, "I guess you were right. Let's add a little to your dry weight," and she left the room. No apology. Just another day at the office! Not for me, it wasn't! I made a mental note: although doctors and support staff are in charge while in hospital, one needs to always advocate for themselves—because no one else will!

7

BEING THE EXAMPLE

I went looking for Him
And lost myself;
The drop merged with the Sea
Who can find it now?
Looking and looking for Him
I lost myself;
The Sea merged with the drop
Who can find it now?

~ Kabir

"Mr. Johnson, we have a heart for you…"
"Woo hoo!" Pandemonium! "Finally getting out of here!" I thought. This was the second time I'd heard those words. Attendants came, moved me onto a gurney, wheeled me through the halls to the elevators, and then down into the belly of the hospital. Many don't know, but there are *catacombs*, tunnels, that run beneath the hospitals. Mount Sinai was on University Avenue, the Toronto General Hospital was across the street, on the corner of University Avenue and Gerard Street, and Sick Kids Hospital was on the other side of Gerrard Street. They were all situated at the T-intersection of University

and Gerard, with Princess Margaret Hospital a stone's throw from Mount Sinai on the same side of University. I would be travelling underground, beneath University Avenue, to the Toronto General Hospital. That's where the transplants were done. There, I would have my chest and torso shaved, get prepped for the surgery, and then lie there and wait...What were we waiting for? With a *cadaveric* (from a deceased person) kidney, surgeons check the suitability through blood work prior to removing it from the donor. However, for a cadaveric heart, they must wait until the organ is removed from the donor, in order to slide their fingers along the coronary arteries on the outside of the heart, to check for coronary disease. If, to the touch, the arteries felt smooth and supple like cooked spaghetti—good to go! But if they felt a little crunchy, like uncooked spaghetti—no go!

Well, another no-go. (*Sigh*) Both times, there was a heart and kidney available together. Not completely sure why I couldn't have the kidney if the heart was no good. Maybe my cardiomyopathy-riddled heart wasn't strong enough to do the kidney surgery alone? Or, maybe, someone was a higher priority for a kidney transplant alone, and I was only high priority if I got both. Who knew? There was a lot of politics surrounding the process. Politics that I wasn't privy to. Anyhow, if I could get a *combo*, that's what I wanted. Both together. *Cheeseburger and fries...and supersize that!*

"When would I get my turn?" I pondered. More importantly, "Why would I get my turn?" Why do some people live, and some people die? I had heard stories that some unfortunate souls didn't get a transplant in time. Then there are the ones, like the kid, that get one, and it rejects, or they died in surgery. What could I do to help ensure that I got a good matching heart, that didn't reject, and allowed me to get back to a normal, productive life? I spent a great deal of time contemplating, "What could I do to stand out from the rest—to be important enough for God to keep me alive?" I meditated strongly on this question, and it came to me, "I would be willing to tell people about what I've been through; I would become an example, *the example*, for people to follow. Yeah, that's it! That's the ticket." That night, I made an unbreakable pact with God, that I would do just that: be the example!

I lived at the hospital for a long time—six months! I watched as the staff and visitors came in heavy coats and boots, then light jackets and galoshes, then sun tans and short sleeves. For me, the conditions were always the same. With the dobutamine working, I felt good overall. I worked hard to deal with my anger, discontent, and need to blame others for my problems. I was welcoming more peace and calm into my daily life. I had also become so thin and flexible that I found it easy to sit in the lotus position (cross legged with feet on top of the thighs like a pretzel); this was a feat I found nearly impossible in the past, but that day I was somehow able to do it. As I stilled my mind and body, I became peaceful and at one with my surroundings. The typical din at the nurse's station had somehow quieted down, and although the large sliding door was closed, it's almost as though I could hear the nurses talking…Quietly…I couldn't really hear words or sentences, yet still tuned in to the talking… About something… About me? Somehow, I knew the sliding door was about to open… And then it did…"Mr. Johnson, we have a heart for you!"

There's a whole team involved in a transplant surgery, so I'm not sure who told me *there was only a heart available*. I was high-enough priority on the waiting list that I became eligible to receive organs from out-of-province. It seemed the MORE Program (Multiple Organ Retrieval and Exchange) didn't have dibs on the accompanying kidney. "I know you wanted both organs, but don't give this one up. It's a big heart, which you need to fill the space vacated by your own enlarged heart. It's in great shape. Time is running out. You should take it"! Okay, yes, I did want both organs, but I wasn't fool enough to pass this one up. I agreed, and the process continued: shaving, prep, extra intravenous lines in, the whole nine yards.

Next, I found myself lying on the gurney, just outside the operating room doors. My family had been called and everyone, who could be, was there. I looked up at the faces that surrounded me. They all looked so concerned. "Did some think they may never see me again? Nonsense!" I thought. "Don't worry," I consoled, "I'll see you in a little while." I tried to put them all at ease, and I meant it. I had great confidence in my surgeon, Dr. R. J. Cusimano, having liked him when I met him a couple of times. Still, something inside gave me the strength and fortitude to know that I was going to survive the operation. There was never any doubt in my mind. I was going to make it. I went in…

On July 19, 2000, I woke up to find myself in the recovery area—*with a new heart!* I had multiple tubes coming out of my body: the ones coming out of my nose carried some kind of disgusting, green bile; a bigger one down my throat, the intubation tube, was for breathing; and two smaller tubes located near my diagram, beneath my pectoral muscles, were for drainage. I also had the ever-omnipresent round stickers, connected to the monitor—via the multicoloured wires—that recorded my vitals. First off, I was glad to still be alive! "Yes!" *Alive and Kicking*, as goes the lyrics to the 80s song by Simple Minds. I can't really say that I was in a lot of pain; they had me drugged up quite well. By the time I was fully cognizant of my surroundings, I realized I was in a critical care unit, a double-occupancy room. A curtain separated me from my neighbor, who also had a heart transplant, and we were both attended to by the same nurse.

I lay quietly in the bed, watching an amazing psychedelic show. No, there was no television or video screen in my room. Still, faces, bodies, and groups of people passed by my vision like ghosts, specters, from another dimension. "Was I dreaming?" No. Strangely enough, my eyes were wide open. As a waking vision, random, normal people wouldn't seem like a strange phenomenon to anyone, but what was strange was that some of them had multiple heads, and these heads were moving and morphing into larger ones, and different ones, and more heads… It's like I was caught up in some bad acid trip or *Pink Floyd* animation. Still, it felt to me as though I should know who these people were, but I did not. More faces were morphing, rising, and falling in front of my eyes. It's almost as if they were trying to tell me to pay attention to what was going on. Deep inside, intuitively, I felt as though the message being broadcast was, "These are all friends of your heart donor; these are his hopes, dreams, as well as his fears that you must exorcise now, so that they don't come to haunt you later." With that realization, came peace. "Bring it on!" I internally dialogued with the entities, "Show me whatever you want! I am not afraid"

Of course, I dare not tell my nurse or any doctors what I was seeing. I already knew what their reply would be: "You're on some pretty strong painkillers, and hallucinations can be a side effect..." I could not deny the possibility that these might have been hallucinations, but at the time, they were very real. I was also connected to these entities in some instinctual way, and that verity could not be explained away as hallucination. Truth is, while it was all happening, I was conscious enough to ask myself, "Is this a dream? Am I hallucinating?" The answers were unequivocally, "No!" So, tell me? If you're in a dream, and you ask yourself, "Am I dreaming?" do you not wake up? Well, I did not, and the show played on, and on, as long as it needed to.

Where did those visions come from? Were they memories, or experiences, buried deep inside the cells of the donor heart? Who's to say? My feeling was that, whether cellular or energetic, those memories, or discorporeal forms, were attributable to the heart donor and not to myself. That message was loud and clear. All cellular memory aside, *someone else's heart* was now my heart. I looked at it like this: when they wheeled me into the operating room I had a heart in my chest, albeit weak and insufficient, there was a heart there nevertheless; when I woke up in the recovery room, I had a heart in my chest, just the same. Outwardly, what had changed? Yes, this new heart was beating strongly and much more rhythmically, but when I glanced down at my torso, it looked roughly the same as it did before—minus the scars.

With the intubation tube down my throat, I couldn't talk. I could only make grunting and murmuring sounds to respond to the nurse, or to direct her to the things that I needed. This technique didn't work well, and I was given a pen and a pad of paper to write the things I needed. I was doing my best to breathe normally but found that I couldn't get a full breath. I wrote to the nurse that I couldn't breathe fully. "It's okay Mr. Johnson, just relax. You need to keep the intubation tube in a little longer. Everything is working fine. You're getting enough air." I was at her mercy; I let it go. Later in the day, Lorie came to visit. She was elated that I'd survived the surgery and I was happy to see her, but there wasn't much conversation to be had. I did, however, relay to her the same issues I was having regarding breathing. She spoke to the nurse about the problem but was sent away in much the same manner as I had been. What really annoyed me, when shift change came, the outgoing nurse told the incoming nurse that I was somehow *a problem patient* for insisting that I was not able to breathe.

The next morning, when the doctor made his rounds, I complained once again. The doctor looked around, checked some equipment readings, then said to the nurse, "This patient can't breathe. Let's get this tube out right away!"

"Vindicated!" I thought, as they prepared to remove the tube. Albeit a quick process, it was a horrible feeling to have this long, accordion-like, plastic tube hauled out of my throat from my lungs. "Ahhhhh!" I sucked the air in in deeply. It felt great to be able to take deep, normal breaths again. Maybe it was due to the pranayama—deep breathing exercises—I practiced regularly, along with my meditation, that caused me to breathe deeper and require more air than average. Who knew? It just felt great to breathe fully again. My thoughts ran back to the nurse from the night before. "Useless twit! She was supposed to be there to help my recovery, not hinder it!" I thought. All I could do was chalk another one up to advocating for myself while in hospital. A work in progress...

"Mr. Wilson! What are you doing? You know you're not supposed to be drinking that," the nurse chastised. "The doctor won't be very happy with you!" Trouble in the neighbouring camp. Mr. Wilson, a man in his late 50s, behind the curtain in our recovery room, had been warned the day before not to drink any type of soda pop. Yet, he was at it again, caught doing the same thing. Seems like his family was sneaking it in for him.

"It's what I like. I don't like water, never have. I've drank a couple of these every day, almost my whole life. I don't think I can stop, and besides, I don't really want to!" Mr. Wilson lamented.

"Seriously?" I imagined. "Dude! What are you thinking? You just got a brand-new heart, a new lease on life, and you're throwing it away for pop? Where's the willpower?" I supposed that he, much like myself, needed to abandon many of the bad habits built up in life. That's why we were here, wasn't it? Our lifestyles needed a total overhaul. We were given a second chance, with this new life-saving organ, and its fate would end up the same as ours if we were unwilling to change. That much I knew. I didn't like to be pessimistic but couldn't get it out of my head that if this guy didn't change, he wasn't going to make it. "*But for the grace of God, there I go!*" This was a mantra that I'd recently taken up saying. I used it when I saw something I didn't want to happen to me, but also didn't want to judge. It was a reminder that it could easily be me, and a way of showing gratitude to God that it wasn't. Amen.

"What a great day!", I thought. My heart had been weak for so long and now it was *tickety-boo!* Working just fine; all on its own, with no sign of the dobutamine pump. "Free at last!" Just then, the door creaked open, and what I saw almost took my breath away. The dreaded dialysis machine was being wheeled in. My heart sank! With all the hullabaloo and goings-on, I had totally forgotten about not receiving the matching kidney, to go along with my new heart. I still needed dialysis to clean my blood and remove the excess fluid. "Nooooooo!" I screamed internally. A teardrop rolled down my cheek.

The heart transplant had taken place at the Toronto General Hospital (TGH), and so did the recovery. I was recovering well, but before there was any thought of me getting out, I had to have a heart biopsy. I was taken to the TGH Cath Lab, much like the one at Mount Sinai. In this procedure, the doctor would run a long, thin, catheter into my heart to check for the pressures in my heart, and secondly, to pinch out a few pieces of heart muscle tissue to be sent to the lab for analysis, looking for any rejection. The procedure was very similar to an angiogram, except in an angiogram, the doctors typically used a groin entry, feeding the catheter up through an incision on the inside of the thigh—where the thigh meets the torso. For the heart biopsy, the incision is made into a blood vessel in the neck, and the *bioptome* part of the catheter is inserted through a sheath and threaded into the right ventricle of the heart. Seemed simple enough...but it could be a painful experience, depending on which doctor was performing the procedure. Imagine lying on a table in a skimpy gown, in a cold room, shivering. Next, you're asked to turn your head to the left to expose your neck. Then a doctor covers you with a papery cloth that has a round hole in it, so only your neck is exposed. It's like covering your head with a blanket, except that your head is near the edge so you can breathe. Then comes the long needle into that sensitive area of your neck, to inject the freezing compound. After a few minutes to let the freezing take hold, you feel a small cut being made and then the sheath being shoved down through your neck, to the sound of, "zip, zip, zip..." as the bioptome passed through the sheath. Then, a strange tickle inside your heart; you feel it flutter when it gets introduced—not a fun feeling! Finally, the *click and pull,* as a chunk of your heart muscle tissue is removed. The process is repeated until four or five pieces of your heart have been taken out for testing. After that, the catheter gets hauled out, and you are asked to help by pressing gauze onto the puncture site, until the bleeding stops, and a Band-Aid is put in place. *A walk in the park!*

I soon came to understand, that these biopsies would be a regular thing. Once a week, while in hospital, then every two weeks after discharge *for a period,* then monthly *for a period,* quarterly *for a period,* semi-annually *for a period,* then, after a couple of years, you could graduate to once a year—*of torture!* I say, *for a period,* because while there was a hospital protocol, it could be altered, longer or shorter, on the advice of the transplant team.

Yes, you would eventually graduate to once a year, but if they had to change your antirejection medicine protocol for any reason, you could get put back on the treadmill of more frequent biopsies again. Speaking of antirejection meds, I now had to take them for life. Antirejection meds were needed to suppress the body's immune system to prevent it from recognizing your transplant as a foreign entity and attacking it, causing the organ to reject. "I did not want that!" They started me off with cyclosporine and CellCept a.k.a. mycophenolate and prednisone. The cyclosporine pills were huge, grey-coated, gel caps that stunk like Heineken beer. Aside from that, I was now getting used to taking a boatload of pills every day, at multiple times during the day. I was also started on some serious antibiotic meds: valganciclovir to prevent CMV (cytomegalovirus) that could occur after an organ transplant; and septra (sulfamethoxazole-trimethoprim), a daily antibiotic to help prevent pneumonia and other infections, due to being immune suppressed.

I now had a whole team looking after me, *the transplant team*, but primarily, I was seen by Dr. Heather Ross. I liked her. She explained things well and made no bones about the direction she thought was best. From what I could see, she was highly respected among her peers, and although I was unfamiliar with the hierarchy at TGH, I felt like I had the *cream of the crop!* Amazingly, after having lived at Mount Sinai for six months awaiting the transplant, after only thirteen days at TGH, I was discharged. Released!…but I couldn't go home. Peterborough was too far to travel to be readily available for the biweekly biopsies. Secondly, having been away from Peterborough so long, I lost my spot at DMC for dialysis. "Total bummer!" I had to remain close to TGH to attend their dialysis clinic—three times a week. I stayed in Toronto with my mother. She had relocated to a different apartment: down the street on Thorncliffe Park Drive from the one I had stayed in before. *Paroled, but still under house arrest—electronic ankle bracelet to boot!* Still…twas good to be out!

8

ONE LUMP OR TWO

Thought is a force, even as electricity or gravitation. The human mind is a spark of the almighty consciousness of God. I could show you that whatever your powerful mind believes very intensely would instantly come to pass.

~ Lahiri Mahasaya

"What is that? Have you noticed that before? Is that new?" I asked Lorie as we lay in bed at our home in Peterborough, just having returned home from Toronto, after being away for close to eight months.

"It's nothing. It's just fibrous tissue. I've always had it. I have some in both breasts. See..." Lorie countered, as she tried to show me other spots on her breast that had a similar, *uneven* consistency, below the surface, to the touch.

"Those aren't the same. And not as big as this one! You need to get that checked out!" I replied.

Sure enough, the lump *that was "nothing,"* was a malignant lump: a tumor. Breast cancer, they were calling it. With this type of discovery, the doctors moved fast! Before we knew it, a surgery was scheduled for a lumpectomy and it was removed, along with several lymph nodes near her left armpit. After the lump was biopsied, we were told that it tested positive for a protein called *human epidermal growth factor receptor 2* (HER2). The doctor informed us that, "In HER2-positive breast cancer, the HER2 gene creates HER2 proteins, or receptors. These receptors, normally, help control the growth and repair of breast cells. But, an over-production of HER2 protein causes *out-of-control* reproduction of breast cells—tumors." He then went on to add, "Chemotherapy is an effective treatment; however, a new immune-targeted protocol is being tested. Would you be interested in that?" There was no question in her mind, Lorie wanted in! Shortly thereafter, we were informed she was chosen to be part of the study. Added to the chemo, was a drug called Herceptin. Herceptin worked by attaching itself to the HER2 receptors and blocking them from receiving growth signals and stopping the growth of the breast cancer. It also caused the immune system to destroy the cancer cells it was attached to.

"What more can happen?" I lamented. "Barely through the door, and now this." We did our best to live as a normal couple, complete with a wonderful son that had just passed his first birthday. We were grateful though because, in the year prior, before my transplant incarceration, we had bought a cottage in Marmora and Lake Township, northeast of Havelock. Now, this cottage was our family retreat as we both battled new, and ongoing, sickness every day. Our little piece of heaven!

The cancer was aggressive! Before we knew it, the cancer had regrown in the left breast, necessitating its removal; then, it appeared in her skin in the chest area and moved into the right breast, likewise necessitating its removal. It also appeared on some scans that it was moving into the bones of her legs. It was slowly consuming her. Still, we pressed on with the Herceptin and other chemotherapy drugs that were added to the mix. The treatments were given at the old St. Joseph's Hospital in Peterborough. The hospital had all but closed down, except for the cancer unit and a few other departments. What a pair we were, juggling her chemo at Saint Joe's, and my dialysis, now back with DMC on Anson Street, near Water Street.

That was about to change. While doing dialysis in Toronto after my heart transplant, I met a lot of great doctors and nurses. One of the nurses told me of a new program that was unfolding: dialysis patients could have a dialysis machine in their home, be trained how to operate the machine, and do their dialysis overnight while they slept. At that time, it seemed too good to be true. The dialysis machines were about $30,000 a pop. "How could it be more cost-effective to have one of those in your own home?" I thought to myself. But somehow it was, and I was accepted into the program. One caveat was that I couldn't be trained on the machine alone; I had to bring someone to act as a backup. At the time of the offer, Lorie agreed to fill the role, but given the series of events that unfolded since I returned home, it was an unreasonable request. Now, I might lose this once-in-a-lifetime opportunity.

With myself on LTD, and Lorie also taking time off work, we were a little strapped for cash. It would've been 60 bucks per round-trip, three times a week, equaling 180 bucks weekly, for six weeks! Thank goodness, there was a program offered by Greyhound at that time, for anyone travelling to Toronto for medical purposes. Even though I was travelling to TGH for training, I was also receiving dialysis there, three times a week, as part of the training, so I qualified. I had to get up early in the morning to catch the bus to Toronto and was super grateful that the destination bus terminal was only two blocks away from TGH. When I showed up for the training, the nurse trainer asked me where my backup was, and I made an excuse that she was ill and couldn't make it that day. Once I got going in the training, I explained what was going on at home, and was allowed to continue on my own. *Phew!*

We were taught how to operate the machine, mix the solutions, attach the dialyzer and hoses, and emergency procedures—the whole kit and caboodle! In the final weeks, we also learned how to cannulate our own fistulas. Once, at DMC, a female traveller came to visit, and she cannulated her own fistula for the treatment. I watched in awe, thinking, "I could never do that!" Now, I had to learn! In the past, at the hospital and at DMC, the nurses poked a new hole every time. For home hemodialysis, we learned what is called the *buttonhole technique*. This technique required two *entrance* holes, and two *exit* holes, to be made in my fistula. You inserted one cannulation needle into entrance hole A, and another into exit hole A, for the first treatment. On the second day, you used entrance hole B and exit hole B. By the third day, scabs had formed over the "A" entrance and exit holes; then you used sterile tweezers to remove the scabs (barf!) from the "A" holes and cannulated those holes again. The next day, remove the B scabs…and you get the idea. I know it sounds disgusting and gross, but the scar tissue of the insertion holes gristled up and created tiny tubes; these tubes acted as guides for the needles to pass smoothly in. At first, I didn't think I could do it, but it's surprising what you can do when you must!

We had to have some renovations done to the house to install sufficient plumbing and the proper electrical power supply in our master bedroom. Then came the dialysis machine and the supplies. This was the first of many large transport trucks that would pull up in front of the house to deliver all that was needed to do my own dialysis at home. I had to clear a spot and put down wooden skids in the basement for box, after box, of supplies. Instead of dialysis three times a week, we were allowed to do it— at a much slower pace— overnight, six times a week, taking Sundays off. I was getting dialyzed so well, my blood work showed minerals were being leached out that normal dialysis patients were supposed to avoid consuming. As such, I was told to eat more—almost anything I wanted—and since I was dialyzed daily, I wasn't so concerned about my fluid intake restrictions. I was beginning to feel healthier and stronger. This was one of the periods when I was up, but Lorie was down.

I was feeling so good that when the person on the other end of the phone said "…We have a kidney for you. Would you be able to come in?" I had to pause for a moment as thoughts raced through my head: "I feel good and healthy, I'm able to eat a normal diet, drink all I want…Do I really want to go through another operation? Being back in the hospital, being under the thumb of the doctors and nurses, the anaesthetic, the cutting, the pain, can I suffer all of that again?"

"Hell yeah!" I'd been chained to a dialysis machine now for over five years. Time to cut and run!

Lorie was feeling well enough to accompany me, and we drove to TGH and checked in on January 17, 2003. I received my kidney transplant at 9:30 AM the next morning. The donor kidney (cadaveric) was placed in my left lower abdomen, near my left leg; its blood vessels were connected to the blood supply in the lower part of my abdomen, and its ureter (urine tube) was connected to my bladder. Many think your old kidneys are removed but removing them is very risky and can lead to unnecessary complications; they were left in place. A kidney transplant is not as intense as a heart transplant and my recovery moved along much quicker. I knew the two most important things after having surgery were: having a bowel movement, and getting out of bed to begin moving, walking if possible. The incision was about six-inches long, and its placement made it very painful to move.

That didn't stop me. A quick blast of the morphine pump and I was up, out of bed. One lap around the nurse's station and utility rooms, two laps, three…This was getting too easy. Walking the halls, I came across a stationary bike and hopped on. A doctor came by and was delighted to see my progress but also cautioned me not to overdo it. I couldn't help it, I felt great. I had done the home hemodialysis for about a year and was grateful I had been chosen for that program; it's what got me strong enough for this transplant. Everything was great, except for one thing—the new kidney wasn't producing any urine. The kidney went into shock after the transplant and stopped producing urine.

Once I got out of the kidney transplant step-down unit and into my own room, I was determined to get this new kidney to work. The surgeon told me, "During the operation, as soon as the kidney was surgically attached, it made urine," so I knew it wasn't a dud. It wasn't going to reject. I had one of those pee-bottle jugs beside my bed. Since I wasn't making any urine, I had to go to the dialysis unit to remove my toxins and fluids. Only, this time around, there was a bonus: no nurses digging the cannulation needles in too deep. I was allowed to put my own needles in, using the buttonhole technique. Sweet!

Daily, I recorded my ins and outs: how much fluids I had taken in, and how much urine I passed out, in the jug. I focused on that jug, like it was a meditation, and *pretended* I could see the jug filling up. First day, 100 mil—barely anything—second day, 200 mil, third day 350 mil, and so it went until I was able to fill that jug over the course of the day. Somewhere, in all that, I stopped pretending and was actually filling the jug up...with biologically generated, new-kidney-graft-facilitated pee! I was ecstatic! After all, I hadn't peed for nearly 5 years! The kidney was finally working and, before long, I was given the green light—no more dialysis! Hooray! Drop the confetti! *End of an era!*

One day, I met a man of East Indian descent in one of the adjacent rooms. He'd also just had a kidney transplant. Maybe he'd received my matching kidney from the same cadaveric donor? Who knew? I had seen him walking in the halls with his wife. He asked me how I was doing, and I told him I was doing well, that my kidney didn't make urine to start but was now beginning to produce normally. I asked him how he was doing? He then went on to tell me a bit of a horror story. His kidney transplant did not take and was already rejecting. He was waiting to hear when they would be doing the follow-up operation—to remove the rejected organ. Then, his wife chimed in and stated, "He has now become diabetic, as a result of the surgery."

"Probably due to the high doses of prednisone," I thought to myself. Then, I could smell it: the rejected organ inside him was beginning to break down and rot. Even though it was inside him, I could still smell it. I felt very sorry for this man. The transplant didn't take and now he was diabetic for life. It showed me, once again, that there weren't always success stories in the transplant world. I was one of the lucky ones.

My mother and my sister Paula had come to visit one evening. My mother was cracking jokes, as usual, and we were having a wonderful visit. It was beginning to get late, around the time for my evening medication to be brought to me by one of the nurses. The nurse came in and started cracking open blister packs and little plastic baggies with medication in them. I looked down at some of the meds that didn't look familiar to me. "Are you sure those are mine?" I asked.

"Yes, they're yours, and it's time to take them," she replied.

"No. They don't look like mine. I make a point of knowing what meds I'm taking, and this is not them," I replied.

"Okay. So, you're saying that you're not going to take your meds? I'll have to report this to the doctor," she said in a frustrated voice, and stormed out.

Paula and my mom looked at me quizzically. "What was that all about?" Paula said.

"Who knows. Those weren't my meds and I'm not really sure who that nurse was," I replied. Within a few moments, the nurse that I recognized from earlier in the day came into the room.

"Oh...I'm so sorry Mr. Johnson. That nurse was just covering for me while I was on break. There's another Johnson down the hall and so there is some confusion with the meds," she went on. She started opening the packages for my medication and I recognized these were the meds I was used to; I took them straight away.

"Good that you know what you're taking," my mother said, "Good that you stood up for yourself!"

In the hospital, or otherwise, there was always a balance to be maintained. One had to constantly fight for recognition and positioning in life, while simultaneously learning to still the mind and quiet a never-ending stream of thoughts to find peace, happiness, and joy. The hospital was a tough place to be to find that balance. People admitted here were fearful of losing the body: their corporeal form. That's why they were in the hospital; but was it really doctors, nurses, scalpels, and sutures—and don't forget the pharmaceutical drugs—that fixed up and healed the body? Or was there something else? Something deeper, more subtle, more elusive, that keeps us alive. I think there is. When I thought my kidney wasn't going to work, I didn't just sit there disappointedly, begging God to come down from heaven and save me. I acted. I used my God-given willpower to exert pressure on that kidney to begin working, and to the rest of my body, to recover more quickly. Another universal law is the *Law of Attraction*—that which we focus upon, becomes our reality. What we think, what we say, and what we do all play a part in manifesting our reality. My mind ran back to Dr. Adams prediction: that it was now up to me. I was beginning to understand what he meant by that.

I used reiki on my new kidney every day, and as I laid my hands on it, I could feel the warmth building up in my palms as the energy was transmitted through my skin, to the new organ underneath. I also meditated, sitting at the side of the bed. It wasn't necessary to sit in the lotus posture. Sitting upright on a chair, or at the side of the bed, was acceptable. Through Self-Realization Fellowship (SRF), I was also taught a technique which called for the use of a wooden T-bar, to rest your elbows on, while you placed your fingers in specified positions (a mudra) on your face and ears, to listen for the sound of Aum—the sound of creation. Since I didn't have my T-bar with me, I raised up the level of the hospital eating tray, so I could rest my elbows on it, and assumed the prescribed posture for the Aum technique. I settled into the technique, and was enjoying the soothing sound when a thought came across me to open my eyes. Sure enough, there was Dr. Ross from the heart transplant team, standing there, staring at me. I could have been embarrassed, but I was not. She knew I was into holistic healing and metaphysics. She looked at me and said, "I'm not even going to ask."

Dr. Ross and I chatted briefly. She was happy that the kidney transplant was a success, and that, although I had to do dialysis for several days, she was satisfied with my new urine output; I would be discharged soon. Seeing as anti-rejection drugs and antibiotics had to be ramped up for the surgery, it would be necessary to do additional follow-up biopsies: to ensure that the heart was not affected. At this point, my biopsies were now up to a year apart; now I had to check my heart health more frequently, again, to ensure all was well after the kidney transplant. "Back on the treadmill," I thought, but in the end, it was well worth it. I was getting my life back. Okay…Some of it…

9

EXPECT THE UNEXPECTED

*When boisterous storms of trials shriek and worries howl at me, I
drown their noises, loudly chanting God, God, God!*

~ Paramahansa Yogananda

"I don't think he's going to say it's in my brain, do you?"
Lorie hoped, as she asked me the question.

"No, I don't think he will." I quickly replied: both to
calm her down from the frightening possibility, but also to hide
my sneaking suspicion the cancer had, indeed, travelled to her
brain. Lorie had been complaining about severe headaches and
trouble with her vision for some time. After scans and tests were
performed, we were awaiting the outcome. My intuition was getting stronger. Sometimes, it helped to have a strong feeling about
what was going to happen next, but it could also be a curse. Some
things you just didn't want to know—and this was one of them!

The waiting seemed never-ending…but after a short while…
we went in to see the doctor. Motionless, we received the dreadful
news that the cancer had metastasized to her brain. Furthermore,
it was located in an area of her brain that made it *inoperable*!
There was silence for a few moments: a brief silence, yet so
expansive you could've travelled to one end of the galaxy, and

back. "What would this mean?" "What do we do?" "Where do we go for answers?" All these thoughts were flooding through our minds, like the tributary branches of the Amazon during rainy season. The doctor did his best to allay our fears, and give suggestions as to next steps, but from where we sat, it was all moot. We thanked him and left.

Lorie's hair had grown back, having lost it during the Herceptin and chemotherapy treatments. She was also back to work. She loved her job as the Head of Human Resources for Kawartha Credit Union. She felt that keeping herself buried in work took her mind off her ongoing health problems. There was no question she could've taken long-term disability, and left work to enjoy the remaining part of her life, but she wouldn't think of it. The credit union was expanding into other cities; and even with her struggles, Lorie was one of the leaders in the expansion effort.

This was also a time of expansion for me. After the kidney transplant incisions had healed, and a modicum of strength returned, it was time to head back to the gym—a place I hadn't been in years. When I first moved to Peterborough in 1991, working out and staying fit was a big part of my life. The YMCA was my go-to spot, and where I first met many local folks. Previously, working out, and more specifically bodybuilding, was a big part of my life. In the years prior to relocating to Peterborough, I could be found seriously cranking up the weights, and blowing up to 260 pounds; then I dieted down to 220 and entered competitive bodybuilding competitions in 1988. I did pretty well back then: placed second in an invitational competition, placed third in the Southern Ontario regional competition, and qualified for the Ontario championships. That was enough for me! A brief, but fruitful, competitive experience. What I was interested in now was health and fitness. No more 18-inch guns and 27-inch thighs! Weight training was a means to get grounded. Whenever I was troubled, or times were tough, the gym always helped me settle down; brought me back to earth. I needed that now.

It also looked like I wouldn't be returning to work. Revenue Canada, now CRA, Customs and Revenue Agency, wanted to fill the spot I left in 1997. I had no interest in returning to that work. I formally retired on October 19, 2005. What I did have interest in, was learning more about metaphysics and holistic healing. Part of me was drawn to the channels in the body through which the energy flowed—*the Chi.* I signed up for an acupressure certificate course in Bolton, Ontario. It was quite an undertaking, not only the daunting idea of going back to school, but also because I had to travel each weekend for ten weeks: two hours to get there, do the course material work, then two hours back home. It was worth it! I learned how to stimulate specific acupressure points—*acupuncture, without the needles*—to relieve the body's suffering from various conditions. I saw myself becoming a holistic health practitioner, and the acupressure would be a big part of that.

I also felt a draw to go deeper with my reiki training. I completed reiki Level Two with Bernie: a one-on-one teaching in which I learned how to use the reiki symbols—more energy, mental clarity, and distance healing—within my treatments. Not only did I have to learn them, I had to become them, and *be one* with the energy. My success in Level II earned me an invitation to Bernie's practitioners' workshop: a weeklong workshop with a dozen other participants from the US and Canada. It was the *piece de resistance* of reiki practitioner training. The practitioners would work in teams of three; one being the patient, one being the practitioner, and the other being a practitioner's helper and observer. On a given day, you would start in one of those positions, and when the treatment was done, all three parties would report to the group, but also to each other. In doing so, for example, if you were the patient you would know what you felt during the treatment but also give feedback to the practitioner on what you felt from them, and they would describe what they felt or saw when working on you. Lastly you would hear from the observer who watched both: you as the patient but also the performance of the practitioner. After the feedback session, the parties would switch, and you would get a chance to feel what it was like from another perspective…Then feedback session…Then switch again...The days were long, and you were wiped out by the end, having received a few emotion-shifting treatments over the course of the day. Each evening when I returned home, I felt so emotionally drained that I didn't think I could do it again the next day. Then the next day, my energy was somehow, magically, returned and I was ready to do it all over again. Each day, we would change partners, creating a new threesome, and begin again. The power of the workshop was that, we not only had a chance to work on others, but continued our own emotional, physical, and spiritual journey by being the subject of others' practical experience. This is where I met Wayne Adam for the first time.

Wayne was a local police officer, but more than that, he was a gifted psychic medium. Later, I learned he was an accomplished musician, poet, and philosopher, too. I watched in awe as he used his gifts of clairvoyance to guide others to the issues that needed emotional release and healing. "What would be my gift?" I often thought. From his experiences on the table that week, I learned that he had a turbulent childhood, similar to my own, and that the path he was now walking was aligned with mine. We would walk together.

The difference between Wayne and myself stemmed from how we came to be at the same place of realization, at the same time. I came from the *push side* and Wayne came from the *pull side* of, what I like to call, the *Push or Pull Theory of Enlightenment*. The theory suggests that all people eventually come to a spiritual awakening in their lifetime. Some get there sooner, and some later, but on average it seems to occur in the early-to-mid thirties. Some people have to be pushed, by way of illness or life-changing event, while others are drawn to it, like the moth to the flame. I ignored the spiritual side of my life, choosing to focus on mental and physical aspirations. Nothing could have swerved me from that path, except for the illnesses that befell me. I got the kidney disease and still did not get it, so I got the heart thing. I get it NOW! Wayne on the other hand, was fortunate enough to be drawn to metaphysical phenomenon prior to anything manifesting in his physical body. After speaking about this, he mentioned sensing a dark foreboding that something was coming, physically, and this prompted him to examine his life and how he was living it. After the workshop, we remained in touch and came to realize we were both accepted as Reiki Master candidates by our teacher and mentor Bernard Morin.

Becoming a Master candidate was no small feat under Bernie's tutelage. Training was to last no less than one year, and you had to exhibit that you had accomplished *Mastery of the Self*, or self-mastery, before you could ever hope to be master of anything (or anyone) else. Bernie was often known to discourage Reiki Mastery until one was ready to accept the responsibility of the energy and the teaching that, undoubtedly, would follow any true master. In essence, *you had to become the energy*, a real-life vessel for healing.

A little-known fact about working with life force energy, and receiving life force energy treatments, is that once you moved through most of your physical expressions of illness, you began to move through the metaphysical pieces, as well. I first used the energy to heal myself faster and more effectively after both my heart and kidney transplants. I then used it to regain my strength and energy to such levels that I was able to resume rigorous fitness training at the gym, played competitive basketball in three local leagues, and competed in dragon boat racing with other transplant recipients. I then began to develop my own subtle awareness of blockages and disease in other people I worked on. I couldn't explain it, but I could sense where people felt discomfort in their bodies before they told me about it. I began to sense truth and could tell when people were not being truthful about issues surrounding their life; issues that would be later verified through further interaction. I was becoming more attuned with my spiritual self, and it guided me and revealed things I was unable to see before.

I completed my training with Bernie and received my attunement to become a Reiki Master on December 14, 2005, in Newfoundland, on a hill overlooking the Atlantic Ocean, near a lighthouse. It was a deeply memorable experience, spending a week with my Master. It was a time of casting off the student embodiment to become a peer with my Master, and other Masters of *Usui Shiki Ryoho*.

I began to work more closely with Wayne. We took up the practice of monthly reiki exchanges; I would work on him, then we would switch, and he would work on me. We also made a pact to call each other on our bullshit, and not to shy away whenever deep work needed to be done. Using his psychic insight and feedback, I confirmed that I was intended to study healing methods, learn about the meridians (channels) through which healing energy traveled, and to study dreams and their meanings. Spirit had been speaking to me through dreams, and upon awakening, I was simply getting up and forgetting them. As soon as I made an effort to remember them, I was able to recount multiple dreams each night, in great detail, and record them in a daily journal. During the day, I analyzed the dreams to discover their hidden meanings, which began to guide me in my life.

It was around this time that Lorie and my relationship began to falter. I'm not sure how, or why, it happened, but I suspect Lorie's past, and what she perceived was happening now, looked familiar. Her first husband had been ill for a time and she took care of him, but when he got better, he began an extramarital relationship with a co-worker, then left their marriage for the interloper. Now that I'd had both my heart and kidney transplants and was feeling better, I believe Lorie saw that as a harbinger of her past revisiting her again. She began to be suspicious of everything I did. "Why are you so late coming back from basketball?" "Why did it take so long to choose movies at Blockbuster?" "Do you really have to do treatments with Wayne?" The list went on and on. Everything I did was scrutinized, and everything I said was examined for some alternative truth. I never told her of the pact I made to be faithful. I was standing by that, and I wasn't going to let anything get in the way—illness, squabbles, being thought of suspiciously—nothing! I did find it interesting though, that I had finally gotten to a place where I could honor myself and be the good man I knew I could be, but the world wasn't ready to honor me. I suppose I had earned that. Karma at its best!

As time went on, Lorie's cancer progressed. At first, they used radiation to shrink the inoperable brain tumor. Then, one day, lo and behold, the doctors proclaimed that the brain tumor *could be reached* after all; it was no longer inoperable. They were willing to go in and remove it. Off came the hair again, and she was left with a large, S-shaped scar in the back of her head. It was horrible to watch as she was taken apart, piece by piece. I had a sneaking suspicion she thought it was unfair that: when I was sick and in hospital, I made peace with my past and was willing to be whisked away—I'd done enough in this life; but Lorie loved life, had never hurt anyone, had never really been sick her whole life, and now sadly watched as it was all taken away. How was that fair? It seemed I didn't care, but stayed; yet she desperately wanted to stay, but had to go. The last straw was when the cancer began to seep into her lungs, and fluid began to build.

Lorie was now on oxygen, full-time. I found it interesting, although she was quite often upset with me and seemed at times to resent me, she wouldn't let anyone else change her oxygen tank. Not that it was a difficult task, but it had to be done swiftly, so there was no period where she would be lacking oxygen. Albeit small, it was her testament that she still loved me, in her own way. She began having trouble breathing and was admitted to palliative care at St. Joseph's Hospital.

Her family, close friends and I thought this might be it, and took turns staying with her in the hospital. However, Lorie was resilient, she was a fighter and wasn't going to go out without a battle. After a few days of R&R, she was discharged from palliative care and returned home. I had recently gotten over an illness requiring me to return to TGH to recover. Maybe it was just the sickness, but I also felt exhausted being the sole caregiver at home. Yes, Lorie's parents were always around, as well as her best friend, Lorri McCabe, and our house became a revolving door through which helpers came and went never-endingly. It could also have been the constant tearing down, the ongoing berating I had to endure—some earned, but some unmerited. During my stay in the hospital, I also thought about Nathan. He might be losing his mom, but I couldn't allow him to lose me, too. My sickness was diagnosed as *walking pneumonia*. Not necessarily lethal for the average person, but I was immune suppressed. I had to take these things seriously. I had to walk a fine line; I had to be available for Lorie, but I couldn't let her take me out. I had to stay strong!

One day, out of the blue, Lorie decided she wanted to stay at her parents' place. They set up a bed for her in the TV room, at the back of the house. At first, I was a little dumbfounded by this move, but they were a close-knit family, spending any free time they had together. In the end it made sense. Lorie may have also concluded that it was too much for me, given my ongoing condition, to deal with everything at home—and she may have been right.

After being at her parents' place for a few days, I was heading over to visit as I'd done daily since she relocated there, but to my surprise no one was home. I received word that she was back in palliative care at St. Joe's and wanted me to come over, that there was something she needed to tell me. She had recently had a bout of troubled breathing but was able to have it relieved as an outpatient; they used a long syringe to draw out a significant quantity of fluid from her lungs and she felt better. Unfortunately, this troubled breathing had returned. "The doctors told me they can't draw out the fluid like they did before," Lorie recounted sullenly. "There's nothing more they can do. They said I only have *two days to two weeks to live*." Everything ground to a halt…The world stopped spinning, and seconds turned to hours, as I tried to reorganize my thoughts in this new dimensional shift.

"Holy fuck!" I thought. It all seemed so surreal. We'd had so many trips to doctors, cancer centers, radiation clinics, chemo clinics, palliative care, the whole schmozzle, and Lorie always came out okay. Why should this be any different? I understood what the doctors were saying, but was I in denial? Maybe I was thinking about it like I would've for myself: rolling in for that heart surgery, I had no doubt I was going to come out on the other side. I always saw myself continuing on—no matter what anyone told me. Maybe what I always hoped for myself, I was hoping for her, and that blinded me from this inevitable truth? Only time would tell.

The next day I came to St. Joe's for my shift. Lorri McCabe was already there and Lorie's sister, Karen McAllister, was just leaving, having stayed the night. When I entered the room, Lorie had changed so much from the day before. She was much paler and frail looking. It reminded me how much willpower played a part in keeping people alive. When Lorie thought they could inject a needle into her lungs, pull out the fluid, and make everything better again, that kept her going. As soon as she realized nothing more could be done, she let go; let go of the hope that she had held onto for so long. Now that hope was gone. Every time I got near her; she would sit up at the side of the bed with her legs hanging down. Within a few moments, she got tired and lay back down in the bed, but each time she would slide further down the bed. Lorri and I struggled to move her back up again. This happened repeatedly. She was desperate to sit up to meet with me. I spoke to the nurse about giving her something to relax. The nurse informed me she had already been given something, that it was given to her regularly, and its effect would be cumulative; it would eventually reduce this repeated agitation. I stayed with her for most of the day until the evening shift showed up: her sister Karen.

That evening, Wayne and I were supposed to do reiki exchanges. I was going to cancel but then thought I could use the treatment to reduce the massive stress load. I was first on the table. When I was done, Wayne told me that was it for the night, that I needed to save my strength, and it was okay that he didn't get his turn. I was tired, but insisted he takes his turn. Wayne gracefully declined and told me to get a good night sleep. "What did he know that I didn't?" I awoke in the middle of the night to the phone ringing and a message that I should get to the hospital as soon as possible!

When I arrived at the hospital, everyone was quiet. Lorie's father, Don Masterson, was inconsolable. It's been said that no parent should ever have to see their child pass before them. Don was no different. He wasn't prepared to do that either; he left, taking Nathan with him. When I entered the room, Lorie was lying there quietly. Her friend Lorri informed me she could no longer see but that she could still hear quite well. Then, Lorri left the room, leaving us alone together. I sat on a chair and pulled it up as close as I could to the bed, to tell her something. In the most warm, comforting voice that I could muster, I told her, "No matter what you think, I never cheated on you. I was always loyal. It's very important that you know that." She heard me. I know she heard me because she, once again, became agitated and tried to sit up on the bed, beside me. Her sister Karen, her mother, Gail Masterson, and Lorri quickly entered the room to see what all the commotion was about. Once seeing that she was trying to sit up again, they told me that was normal, and had been happening all night. I stood up and positioned myself beside the bed and put my arm around her to get her to lay back down.

Just then I heard her mother say, "Oh my..." In that same moment, Lorie's head fell back in my arms to reveal that her eyes were motionless, now looking up at the point between the eyebrows, the Christ consciousness center. Lorie's soul had left her body. The feeling that came over me next was indescribable—like being punched in the gut at the same moment the ground had fallen out from under me, and I was in freefall. Farther, farther, and farther down I fell. An intense surge of emotion came over me, and I sobbed uncontrollably. The rest of the family entered the room. Her brother, Dan Masterson, who was closest to me, reached out and held me as I bawled like a baby. This was the first time I had ever seen the soul leave a body—and not just any body, the body of my beloved wife. Ultimately, this was all somehow expected, yet, still felt unexpected. Many tears were shed in that room by all.

What happened next, bothered me a little. Lorri and the family began packing up all of Lorie's paraphernalia she had brought to the hospital. I watched as someone set a bag on Lorie's legs and began filling it. She was only dead a few moments, and her body was being used like a table, to pack a suitcase for a trip to some unknown destination. It just seemed wrong to me. Still, I watched as the family worked away busily, like ants clearing the remains of a picnic ground—organized and efficient. Then they were gone, after having returned Nathan to be with me at the hospital. I took Nathan in alone to show him that his mother was no longer with us. He was only six years old, but I didn't want there to be any question as to where his mother went, when he asked later. Now he knew. It was time for us to leave, but leaving felt somehow strange and different. Up until now, every time we went somewhere, we left as a family—three of us. Now, three of us were there, but only two could leave. That's how it would be from now on.

PART III

LIFE LESSONS

2006 - 2015

10

ANGRY BIRDS

*You thank God for the good things that come to you, but you don't
thank him for the things that seem to be bad;
that is where you go wrong.*

~ Ramana Maharshi

"Everything will be okay dad, you will see," Nathan said, as he tried to console me, still reeling from the loss. I was a grown man, and he was only six years old. His mother had just died, and he was telling me it was going to be okay. He was wise beyond his years.

The next day was a different story. I knew I had to pull myself together. Yes, there was still a wake and a funeral to come, but Lorie had, proactively, arranged all of that with her family. They were taking care of it all. All Nathan and I had to do was attend. But today, I was a single parent with a child that had to get to school. We got up early, I made him a warm breakfast—dipping eggs with toast—his favorite, then I took him to school and headed off to the gym. I desperately needed to get grounded. I was now at GoodLife Fitness, in the north end of town, no longer working out at the YMCA. This became our routine.

I continued with my meditation practice through SRF. I had been practicing their flagship meditation discipline, *Kriya yoga*. They called it *the jet plane method to God realization*; the fastest way to get there. Kriya yoga is an advanced technique for spiritual evolution that had been taught by enlightened sages for thousands of years. *Kriya works by giving the practitioner control of their life force. Through life force control, the yogi is able to overcome all the obstacles preventing union with the Divine.*[iv] Each Kriya breath is equivalent to *one year* of spiritual living. I was now practising 36 in each meditation sitting. I was also supposed to be practicing it morning and night, but given everything I had just been through, and now being a single parent, I was only able to accommodate the nighttime practice. I had been practicing 36 for over a year, and it was my expectation to request an increase each year, adding 12 more Kriyas to the practice. I had called SRF to set up an appointment and was now speaking to one of the monks of the order. I explained my situation, my wife's recent passing, and gave an update on my meditation practice, purposely avoiding the issue of the twice daily meditation requirement. Of course, he asked about it, and I could not lie about it. In the end, he told me, "With your present situation, 36 Kriyas is a good number for now. Continue with that until your life settles down, then we can take a look at an increase later."

I was devastated. My spiritual growth meant more than anything, and now life circumstances had ground my progress to a halt, or so I felt. I had my meditation room all set up, with a chair in the middle covered by a wool blanket to block any negative earth currents, my bookshelf was full of spiritually-minded books, I had the beads, the T-bar for the Aum technique, everything; I was doing all of it right, except for the morning meditation. "Could they not see how committed I was?" I lamented. Thirty-six Kriyas was nothing, considering the goal was 108. How was I going to get there if they didn't let me make my yearly increases? Being *angry* about my *spiritual growth* was an oxymoron; I could no longer see the forest for the trees. I was distraught, and I let my anger get in the way of my progress.

Wayne and I continued doing treatments. I needed them now, more than ever! During one of our get-togethers, he spoke about an idea that came to him after seeing a news article about the Chinese prime minister looking like Richard Gere. He showed me the picture, and there was definitely a resemblance. As a police officer, he was familiar with the burgeoning of facial recognition technology (FRT). In those early days, it was predominantly earmarked for law enforcement, airport security, casino security, things of that nature. No one was yet using it to find look-alikes. His intuition told him the idea would be worth millions, and now he was pitching it to me. "I don't know anything about facial recognition technology. That's not for me," I told him. We went on with our treatment exchange.

At that time, the movie *The Secret* was becoming popular. The premise behind *The Secret* was all about the Law of Attraction — that which you focus upon becomes your reality. The show interviewed several successful authors and stars, and each gave tips and tricks on how to manifest a successful life. *The Secret* asked, "What would you do with your time if you had all the money that you needed, and no one to help but yourself?"

"What would I do?" I asked myself. I'd recently taken a couple of art courses in the Charlotte Mews, in Peterborough, and truly enjoyed it. I had a bit of a knack for it—both watercolor and acrylic painting. Whatever art piece I couldn't finish while in the class, I took home. I covered my dining table in newspaper, and continued with it, any moment I had free. It felt like I could do it all day! "That's it! I think I could paint all day, if given the time."

Next, *The Secret* asks, "Once you've chosen what you'd really like to do, how do you fund it?" It further goes on to say, "When you've decided what you want, the universe conspires with you to send opportunities your way to make your dreams a reality. But be careful, if an opportunity comes by and you don't take it, it might be gone forever!"

Then it dawned on me, "I just had an opportunity come by that could be worth millions. Wayne's look-alike idea. Maybe I should look at it a little deeper." I got on my computer, and began researching: Who were the thought leaders on FRT? How much would it cost to license or buy? Who could lend us money? I realized I could do this, picked up the phone, called Wayne, and told him I was in! We got together again, sat down and searched for a name for the business. We needed a name that also had the associated .COM domain name available—that would be important. We found it! The company would be called I Look Like You, and we were able to grab the domain name *ilooklikeyou.com*. We subtitled it: Uniting the World, One Face at a Time. We felt that, in a world of animosity and war, how could you go to war with a country where a person lived that looked *just like you*? Maybe it was a little high-flying, but we liked it. I had also spent a fair bit of time, while I was off work, learning about digital images and graphics and got pretty good with Photoshop. Next, we found ourselves WYSIWYG'ing a logo: a globe containing two profile faces, such that these faces looked like continents facing each other. Perfect!

From then on, all we thought about was ILLY (acronym for I Look Like You). We busted our butts and put together a business plan in time to submit to Community Futures Development Corporation (CFDC) for their next funding round, in the first quarter of 2007. CFDC offered loans to small businesses in the Peterborough area, and their maximum loan product was C$150,000; that's what we went for. Thankfully, we were successful enough in our application to be called before the board. It was a little intimidating, sitting before this group of successful Peterborough businesspeople, both men and women, who grilled us on the workings of our business plan. We would not be deterred; two nobodies from Peterborough and Lakefield, an ex-taxman and a cop, did our little dog and pony show, and guess what? We got it! When I went in to pick up the check from the director of CFDC, she told me that she had spoken to one of the board members, asking, "Do you know what we just gave that money away for? This I Look Like You, thing?"

"Nope. No idea," he replied

I chuckled to myself, "*The Secret* and the universe in action. They didn't even know why they gave us the money. They just knew they had to!" I felt blessed.

For the next year and a half, I became caught up in ILLY: incorporating the business, opening bank accounts, meeting with developers, and launching the first few iterations of the website. The original business plan suggested income would be earned from ads on the site. The site was free, and people inherently had a desire to find their look-alike. We had interest, just no way to keep users engaged and stay on the site. We had the hook, we just needed to make it sticky. The C$150,000 seemed like a lot, but it was gone before we knew it. We needed new investors.

Business, business, business, and little time for anything else. My meditation regimen was slipping away. I was so sure ILLY would hit it big, and quickly, that I even told Nathan, "Daddy doesn't have much time to play because of business. It'll be over soon, and we can play then." My life, once again, became twofold: business and gym. My life triangle was teetering. My social life was non-existent. I had met a few ladies through friends and acquaintances, but nothing that lasted. I wasn't into going out much. The world was becoming more cloistered, more Internet-based. Facebook had just launched, and quickly overtook MySpace as the world's largest social network. Everything was online, even dating. Dating sites were becoming a real possibility for meeting people locally. Reluctantly, I jumped on a site called *Lavalife*, and gave it a whirl. I typed in my likes and dislikes and was presented with a list of potential matches.

I could hear Wayne's voice in the back of my mind saying, "You need a Mona!" Mona Adam was Wayne's wife, and he felt comfortable enough in his relationship to suggest I should find a woman like her. This played in my head, as I met Denise MacDonald through Lavalife. Coincidentally, her birthday was October 15, the same as Mona's. What were the chances? We chatted first, then met for the first time at Riley's, a pub in downtown Peterborough. Denise was an entrepreneur, having cofounded a program that taught kids with Down syndrome and autism how to read, called Out-Of-The-Box Reading (OOTBR). The program saw her travelling regularly throughout North America, doing workshops and presentations, predominantly to the Down Syndrome Association crowds. She had recently left a relationship and had just moved into a home in the north end of town. She also had two kids, Ariana and Melissa, aged 13 and 10 respectively, who lived with her. It was a great first meeting. What topped it off was that she was tall—5'11". Being 6'3" myself, most women I dated, including my past wife, were average height—around 5'7". This was something new to me, and I liked it. We seemed to have hit it off and agreed to get together again.

"Another relationship? What was I thinking?" I was cognizant enough be respectful of anyone associated with my last relationship, and that a certain amount of time between relationships needed to be considered. I was somewhat old-fashioned, thinking that one should not enter another relationship until at least a year had passed beyond the passing of a spouse. I hearkened to the medieval days, when the spouse of the deceased wore black for extended periods of time. Not quite like that, but we all grieve differently, and my hospice training taught me that grieving was necessary and unavoidable; you couldn't run away from it. There was no running, I had done plenty! In addition, my views of death were more aligned with Eastern traditions. In the East, they celebrated death. The deceased are heralded as having escaped this world of trials and suffering to a better place. They got out, and we're the suckers left behind! It was now 2008, almost two years a widower. I gave myself permission to move on.

Denise and I began seeing each other regularly, she travelling to the south end to see me, and I travelled to the north and to see her. Inevitably, as with all expanding relationships, it made sense to combine resources and move in together. Her house was newer, so we chose Carriage Lane. I had lived on Ephgrave Boulevard, and it wasn't lost on me that I was moving from the *grave* to the *carriage*. Typically, the saying goes, "from the cradle (carriage) to the grave," but I was doing it in reverse. I should have picked up on that at the time, but I was no longer looking for messages—as learned in my shamanic work. I had completely stopped meditating. I was engrossed in business, the gym, a new relationship, and potentially a whole new family. "Where was all this taking me?" Only time would tell.

When I first met Denise, she was struggling with some hormone issues, as well as, struggles with back pain. She was taking a whole host of naturopathic herbs and remedies. Her cupboard was full, and she was paying a fortune for them. We decided to go see a friend of mine, Deborah Coulton, another reiki practitioner I met at Bernie's practitioner training. We stayed in touch, and she told me about a man, named Jerry Veldt, who founded a treatment system called Holistic Body Analysis, that she was learning the system from him, and that we should come and see him when he was at her home next, in Stratford, Ontario. I thought, "This might be just the thing to sort out some of Denise's health issues," and we made an appointment to go see him. When we got to Deb's, she was surprised the appointment was for Denise alone, and that I wasn't planning to be seen by Jerry. She gave me one of those looks—a Deb look—that told me something was wrong. When we went in to see Jerry, I was fascinated as he did this funny little tapping with his fingers on Denise's shoulder, while he quietly called out what seemed like a thousand names of vitamins, minerals, organs, glands, etc. He continued and found the problem areas, and the corrective herbs to fix the problems, then relayed them to Deb, who recorded them on an analysis sheet. Finally, he took the analysis sheet and described to Denise what was happening in her body. He went over the symptoms associated with those problems, including the herbs necessary to fix them. He was bang on. "How could he know?" I marveled. When he was done, he looked over to me.

"So, you're the guy that Deb was talking about. You're like a miracle standing here in front of me. I understand that you didn't come for an assessment, but I'm curious. You mind if I do an assessment on you, free of charge?" Jerry asked. How could I refuse? He ran through that long list of things again, while tapping on my shoulder. Then he picked up the assessment sheet Deb had recorded and began reading the details. "Well if I thought you were a miracle before, now I really know you're a miracle," he began. It turned out that one of the items that he called *chemical*, was way out of whack. He explained that there should be zero chemical in the body, but when it hits 11, little cysts, tumors, and fibroids can begin forming. When it hits 30, those things are most likely in the body, and when it hits 50, "you know what" is probably all through the body. My number was 75!

"Oh crap!" I had to confess that I hadn't been feeling well lately. I was starting to get that sickly feeling again, like when my kidneys were first going down, but I didn't want to admit it to myself. Deb gave me that look again, while nodding her head and pursing her lips. I knew what that meant. She had seen it on me when I came in, and now I also knew what she was seeing. Without question, we grabbed the herbs that he was suggesting, paid for them, and never looked back. I dodged another bullet that day; bent over backwards and swayed back and forth, like Neo in *The Matrix*. I was beginning to believe.

Leaving Strafford, I realized we would be passing close to my father's home in St. Clements, Ontario. After my parents split, he got remarried and now had three children—Christina, Jessica, and Stacey—apart from me and my three sisters. My dad and I were somewhat estranged. I tried to reconnect with him from time to time, but it always had to be on his terms, and that didn't work for me. Whenever I'd call, "Hey dad, I'd like to see you. Want to get together for a beer somewhere?" The answer was always the same.

"Not today. Maybe another day, and it would be best if you come to the house..."

So, it just never happened. I had already been to his house, met his wife, Pat, and the kids, stayed for dinner, etc. What I really wanted was a relationship with my father. I never really knew him. "This was my opportunity," I thought. "I'll call him and tell him that we're 20 minutes out and would like to stop by. How can he decline?" I did, and before long we were knocking on the door.

We were greeted by his daughter Jessica, who let us in to the family room where he was seated. Jessica sat with us. My father had been in a severe car accident years ago and was pronounced dead at the scene, but he somehow managed to come back to life, albeit having sustained serious injuries. Of course, the first thing out of his mouth was, "So…you remember where I live, eh? I was wondering how long it would take for you to come around?"

I wasn't having it, and replied, "Dad, my wife died a couple of years ago, and you didn't even take the time to call me." Needless to say, that was the end of the chastisement and he wanted to move on and leave the past in the past. A broken record. It was a short visit; the thrust of the conversation being that my two older sisters and I would like to come and visit him. My sisters, Donna and Paula, struggled to forgive him after a tumultuous family life, ending in his leaving our mother. They were ready to let that go now, and come to see him. He seemed elated, and we agreed it would be the Monday of the following week. Then we left.

At the cottage that weekend, I awoke to a message that my father had died. I wish I could say I was heartbroken, but those feelings left a long time ago. I was more puzzled and stupefied at why he left at this juncture in his life? The weekend before he would finally get to make peace with his first children, why would he disappear into the unknown? Was it too much to handle? Was he that afraid of what he might hear? Why now? I guess I'll never know. I found it interesting that I'd been given a chance to visit him before he passed. Maybe that was enough. At his funeral, they played Bob Marley's *Everything's Gonna Be Alright*. Similarly, the repeating numbers 222 mean the same—to those that follow that type of thing. Every time I see 222 on the clock, on a license plate, or on a billboard, it reminds me that my father is with me, helping me in any way he can, letting me know, "Everything's going to be alright!" *Rest in peace, pops.*

11

PANAMA-AH-OH-OH-OH-OH!

You have been in a state of hallucination thinking that you are a mortal, struggling and suffering.

~ Paramahansa Yogananda

"We have no one to teach grade seven mathematics," Dr. Cabanellas implored. "And that is your son, Nathan's class. If we cannot find an English-speaking math teacher, we'll have to use a Spanish-speaking one, and that will be harder for Nathan."

I knew where he was going with this. Dr. William Cabanellas was the founder and principal of International Charter Academy (ICA), in La Chorerra, Republic of Panama. He was baiting me to take the job. Little did I know, it was not only the grade sevens that were missing a math teacher; they needed one for grades four, six, and eight, as well. "I dragged Nathan here to Panama," I thought. "I can't let him be forced to learn Spanish overnight. I'll have to take the job." I suppose it was my own fault. I shouldn't have let him know that my earliest focus in university was math and science, not to mention, a work history that included accounting and auditing. I was the natural fit. I agreed and took the job.

We moved to Panama for a number of reasons. The idea originally came from my youngest sister, Allison Johnson-Cooper, when we went to visit her in Florida a few months prior. Allison married an American, Carl Cooper. In the early years of their relationship, they were young jetsetters, travelling to, and working in destinations such as Grenada and Vietnam. Now they had an established family with four children—Malayka, Natalia, Ford, and Caliana (later Carlson)—and settled down in a wonderful gated community in Fort Myers, Florida. Allison and Carl, both, spoke highly of Panama, how it was a third-world country becoming more stable, they transacted in the American dollar, and their wireless infrastructure was good— an important requirement for conducting international business. They were planning on moving there and thought it would be fantastic if we joined them. Well...we moved and waited months for them to come... but life changed, and they didn't make it. *Que sera sera!* The second reason in favor of Panama, was to try out eReadingPro, the evolution of Out-Of-The-Box Reading, as an English-as-a-second-language (ESL) program. Denise and her cofounder/partner had a falling out but agreed (after many legal squabbles) that each could use the principle concept of the product, as long as it was rebranded; neither of them was entitled to continue using the name. This was the reason I found myself teaching math. ICA was the English-immersion school Denise had found that was willing to take her on, to try out her ESL program, teaching the grade three homeroom class. Lastly, Panama was great because it was inexpensive to live there. A family could live comfortably on $2,000 a month. With the fall of Out-Of-The-Box Reading, Denise's income followed suit, and I, now on a small pension, didn't bring home enough to make ends meet. So, we boxed up our possessions, shipped what we needed, and rented our home— furnished—to a conscientious pair of young ladies. All was good.

We lived in a small, two-bedroom home in *Las Arboledas*, a gated community across the Pan-American Highway from the town of La Chorerra. We rented from a gracious young man named José Manuel Medica, and grew to be good friends with him and his parents, Manuel Medica Ochy and Blanca de Medica. The family introduced us to Panama, and took us to various cities, and attractions. Friends for life! Back home in Canada, not long after our marriage, Denise's two girls were with their dads. Melissa, who had promised her father she would live with him beginning in high school, moved in with him before we left. Ariana repaired her relationship with her father, and was off to Carleton University in Ottawa, close to Québec where he lived. Travis, who had come to live with us for a while in Peterborough, moved on to work on his music. After buying him a guitar for his 13th birthday, he exploded with musical talent, learning and excelling at both acoustic and electric guitar, drums, and vocals. He played in a number of seminal bands and was now working on a solo career. He appreciated staying with us, but felt he needed to do things on his own, and I supported him in that.

Manuel and his family knew all the best beaches, some hidden off the beaten trails. We remembered our way back to one of those beaches that had a hot spring nearby. On one occasion, friends from Canada were vacationing at a resort in Panama, and we met up with them. They wanted to try something different, so we took them to the hidden beach. It was a hot, sunny day and the water was perfect. "Time for some body surfing!" I proposed. Everyone was in. The waves were fairly strong that day, and I noticed the sand at the shoreline was steep, such that it dropped off quickly when you entered the water. Nathan and I caught a couple of pretty good waves, stiffened out our bodies, and rode the waves in, to the shore. After a couple of rounds, I noticed that we had been dragged down the shoreline, getting close to a rockier part of the beach. I made a point of telling Nathan that it was important we wade back along the shore to where we started, to avoid the rocks. He agreed, and we caught a few more good ones. Foolishly, I hadn't noticed how far toward the rocks I was getting and caught a doozy of a wave. Stretched out inside the wave, I knew I was coming in hot! In that moment, time stood still...I could see my own thoughts. "You're coming in way too fast! What to do? What to do? You're going to hit shore—hard!

And remember, you're heading toward a steep slope. There will be no soft, coasting into the shallow waters. And how close are you to those rocks, you idiot? Fuuuuuuck! The waves have me; no way out. BRACE FOR IMPACT!" I stuck my arms out, keeping them as stiff as I possibly could, preparing to hit shore. Then, CRUNCH! At the speed I was going, my arms folded like a lawn chair, my head hit the sand and the crunch I heard was the vertebrae in my neck being compressed and bent out of shape. "Have I broken my neck," I feared. It felt like I'd been out for a moment. I then realized I was at the beach with friends, so I quickly got up as if nothing happened. I was surprised that I could walk normally and sauntered over to the group. They were standing by our beach towels chatting away, not noticing. Just another day at the beach.

No! It was *not* just another day at the beach. The neck damage from the body surfing accident was taking its toll. It had been days since I was able to sleep. My left ear ached so bad and throbbed constantly; there was no escape from the pain. On top of that, my heart was now doing a funny thump, th-thump, th-thump thump…thump…Strange arrhythmias were setting me off into a panicked state. I got up and paced the house, sometimes pacing the carport outside, driving myself insane with thoughts of dying and leaving my family behind. I don't know why I didn't go see a doctor. A part of me knew they wouldn't treat it as a neck injury, just blow it up into something about my heart, which wasn't how it started. I couldn't go there! It was now 2010, ten years post heart transplant without incident— except for a small coronary artery blockage found in an angiogram just before I left Canada. Small potatoes in the great scheme of things. Since moving to Panama, I had blown off my yearly required visits to the transplant team. It's like I was finally free. Now this. I just couldn't bring myself to return to being a pincushion for the *medical industrial complex.*

One night, I lay in bed, suffering from the pain. I prayed to God that he would send me a blessing, that I wasn't a bad person, and didn't deserve this. God responded. He gave me an *ability*. An ability to nullify pain. While lying in bed, I reached my hand up and touched my left ear…and the pain was gone! I was astonished! "Would it work again?" I posited, then touched the side of my head, above my ear, an area that also ached, and the pain vanished there, too. "Awesome!" Before long, I placed my fingers over every area that had pain, and it left those places, too. Lastly, I placed my fingers over my heart, and to my delight, the raucous thumping subsided. "It's a miracle!" I thought to myself. "What a gift!" Unfortunately, my head got big, and my mind wandered. "This is like the healing power of Jesus, when he healed so many sick, back in the day. I wonder what I'll be able to do with this?" But such things are not the domain of men. After finally getting a good night's sleep, I awoke to find the gift had left me. I wondered whether I had reserved it for myself, would it have remained? Too late now. A lesson in humility.

We didn't stay in La Chorerra for long. After the beginning of the school year, the whole English-immersion thing at ICA was going out the window. We spoke with a number of teachers who had taught there in previous years, and they told us this was the *modus operandi* for the school. Historically, it seemed, English-only speaking teachers were brought in, and kept only long enough, to host teacher night. Long enough for the Panamanian parents to meet the English-speaking teachers, then they were let go. After that, Spanish-speaking teachers were brought in to finish off the year, and they were not concerned with whether the kids were immersed in English at all. At that point, we'd had enough anyway. The school was supposed to have screened the incoming children. The kids needed to know *some* English, in order to have a sporting chance, given ICA used English-only textbooks. Many kids spoke no English at all, and the first round of teachers knew little, to no, Spanish—a shit show! I could totally understand why they brought back the Spanish-speaking teachers. They had no choice. The trouble was, Nathan was still stuck in the school. He had met many new friends and was finding his way—at first! After the teacher swap, I watched, heartbroken, as he tearfully brought his school assignments home in Spanish, translated them with Google translator, completed the work in English, then translated them back for submission. Now, he was the one in Spanish immersion, and he braved it like a champ! He finished the year with a 3.7 GPA, ahead of many of the Panamanian kids that were learning in their own language. Pure willpower!

We moved from La Chorerra, and settled down in a gated, beach community called Coronado. In La Chorerra, we lived in amongst the Spanish-speaking Panamanians, with a mind to immerse ourselves in the Spanish language and culture. In Coronado, however, there were many Canadian, US, and other international ex-pats. Most of them spoke English, so it was less stressful, given that we were not yet fluent in the domestic dialect. Coincidentally, we rented our new home from the director of Panama Coast International School (PCIS), Kathy Kress, where Nathan would attend. The school offered full-English education to students in Panama's Pacific beach communities—a perfect fit.

Now that we were no longer schoolteachers, both Denise and I had to find another way to subsidize our income. Denise made friends with some American ex-pats that started a budding real estate company. Her experience presenting and promoting her reading programs, coupled with a previous stint as an investment broker, made her a shoo-in for selling real estate. I, on the other hand, would set up shop in our newly rented home, providing holistic health services to the ex-pats in the community. Before leaving Canada, Denise was enamored with Jerry Veldt and the Holistic Body Analysis experience at Deb's in Strafford. Jerry offered a training package: books, DVDs, and CDs, that one could study at home, then attend periodic classes whenever he was in Ontario. We bought the package, but it sat there collecting dust as Denise was constantly occupied with the rebranding of Out-Of-The-Box Reading into eReadingPro, travelling and presenting abroad. Of course, I picked the training package up, and ran with it; I couldn't let that money go to waste. In hindsight, was it really for her, or for me all along? I can see Deb giving me one of those looks right now. My little clinic was a success. Panama was great for modest retirees, wanting to live out their days relaxing by the beach and sipping mojitos at the local patio bar. None of that was enjoyable if you didn't have your health. No, I couldn't set your arm if you broke it, or perform an operation. By using muscle testing, however, as well as reading the eyes, ears, teeth, and tongue, I could see disease brewing long before a doctor could give it a name. What I offered was prophylactic vitamins, minerals, and herbs to remedy existing problems and to help keep the body in balance, avoiding *unnecessary visits* to the doctor. Ex-pats could appreciate that. So word travelled beyond our local community and throughout all of Panama that a Canadian was offering holistic services in Coronado. Win-win!

ILLY was also a work in progress. Now on our third iteration of the website, we were looking for investors to really blow it up. While in Panama, I met regularly with our team, wirelessly, that now included three new members: Richard Schumacher, an engineer, entrepreneur, and old high-school friend; Jason Lightfoot, a friend that Richard brought in who understood tech and owned an environmentally friendly, energy-efficient lighting company CONXCORP; and Lyriq Bent, a Jamaican-Canadian actor known best for his roles in the *Saw* films and Canadian TV series *Rookie Blue*. Wayne, Richard, and Lyriq would be travelling to San Francisco to meet with a start-up lawyer and an angel investment team Lyriq had connected us with. Things were looking up, but business was always a roller coaster as each partner had different ideas of how best to move forward. The guys had a lot of ideas—balloons—and I had to be the guy holding the strings that kept them from floating away. Personally, I hated the role, and didn't want to be the one to always burst the bubbles. I voiced this distaste to the team, but they agreed that we needed that grounding from time to time. I kept on, keeping on.

Thinking back to the pain I suffered after the body-surfing neck injury, and the miraculous healing from that pain, I began to wonder whether that healing was only a stopgap measure to buy time to get help. I hadn't done much physical fitness since coming to Panama, so I bought some weights, and tried working out, to no avail. Every time I tried, I would aggravate the soft tissue damage in the neck, and the pain would return. It seemed the quieting of the pain with my fingers, months ago, only allowed my body to strengthen itself *around* the damaged area, throwing everything else out of balance. I was now developing strong pain in my left trapezius muscle and an area behind my left rhomboids. My body was beginning to break down, and no matter what I knew (Holistic Body Analysis, reiki, Muscle Energy Technique or MET), and whatever could manipulate the physical body, I tried. "My body isn't recovering" I thought. "Why not?" My mind ran to my antirejection meds. "These things block my immune system, preventing my body from repairing itself." While I studied science in university—inherently, a science-based guy—I still harbored a lack of trust for the medical establishment. "Did I really need to keep taking antirejection meds for the rest of my life?" I understood that every seven to 10 years, every cell in the body is replaced by a new cell. In other words, we become a brand-new person. Following that reasoning, and the time elapsed since my transplants, I decided that "These organs are now mine; the transplanted grafts should now have been replaced with my own cells. No more need for these draconian drugs." I stopped them. All of them.

One night, I had a dream, and in that dream a voice spoke to me. "You no longer have to worry about your heart. It will be taken care of." I was getting help, again, from on high. God, and my guru, were always with me. A true guru is an avatar; one who had, already, worked through all their earthly karma and sits with God. Knowing the righteous path, they incarnate back on earth to guide us and show us the way. Finding one's guru was a blessing, not only because they lighted the way, but they helped share the burden of the disciple's earthly karma. The guru takes 25% of your karma, the disciple gets 25%, and the remaining 50% is the grace of God. I had totally forgotten about this. Why was I dealing with 100% of this problem when I could reduce it to 25%? After Lorie's death, I let my meditation practice slip away, and could now see the result of my spiritual inactivity. Time to get back at it!

The Coronado *casa* (house) didn't have enough rooms for a separate meditation room, so I bought a portable, accordion-like, wicker separator wall to place my meditation chair and a small altar behind and set it up in a corner of the spacious bedroom. I picked up my meditation regimen full force, day and night, without fail. This practice was all new to Denise. When I first met her, I had already stopped meditating. Now that I was meditating again, I knew that I would change. "How will these changes affect her?" I wondered. "Will she still love me in the same way? I have to tell her what might happen and give her the right to choose. It's only fair." I did. I told Denise that returning to meditation, and my Kriya yoga practice, was the only way to save my life. With the real estate stuff, all the ex-pats milling about, Facebook updates of our lives, etc., we were *out there*! That would change for me, to a life more akin to solitude and reflection. I could understand that she might not want to be a part of that. I was willing to let her go. If continuing with the current way of life was a deal breaker, I would have no choice. "Take some time to think about it," I offered, sympathetically.

"Yes," she replied tearfully. "I don't need any time to think about it. I want to share this new way of life with you." I was happy and grateful for this reply, but a part of me knew it would be difficult for her. Denise loved the spotlight. She'd had the spotlight before, but now the spotlight was conjoined with a life by the ocean, the sun, warm breezes, and a year-round tan. Who could give that up? We shall see.

Life continued, but so did the weakening. I reluctantly began reducing my holistic practice, turning away clients in favor of rest and solitude. At one point, I never left the house for three months solid. People kept asking about me, and we told them that I was having back troubles. The grip in my shoulders, traps, and rhomboids, was like a vice around my heart, squeezing the life out of it. When I would work with clients, I would muscle test something called *life force*. It would tell me *how willing* a client was to work on their own healing. Clients would swear they would do anything to get better, but my life force reading often told me different: they were okay with passing on. I now started taking my own life force reading…and it was coming up 50-50. *A crapshoot!*

Denise's real estate business was in full bloom, along with her responsibilities to get out and do meet-and-greets with new clients. This happened twice a week at the local *Picasso Bar and Restaurant*. The PCIS high school kids hung out there, too, so Nathan would accompany her, leaving me home alone to my own devices. Lately, my heart rate was beginning to increase, now around 120 bpm at rest. This worried me. Still, I had the utmost faith in my beliefs that, somehow, that message in my dream meant that a miraculous healing was on its way. I wanted nothing less than that. In meditation, I learned to slow down the breathing and the heart rate, with the goal of entering a state of samadhi: "…*the devotee's consciousness merges in the cosmic spirit; his life force is withdrawn from the body, which appears 'dead', or emotionless and rigid. The yogi is fully aware of his body condition of suspended animation.*" I was desperate to reach this state, to experience death, while still alive. All of a sudden, I felt a funny feeling. Actually, not a feeling at all. It was more like my heart wasn't there; I couldn't feel it beating anymore. I muscle tested my life force…it was zero! "Oh shit!" I walked over to the bed and lay down with my arms folded across my chest and my hands overlapped, resting over my heart chakra. I lay there and waited to die. Correction: not to die, but to go into that breathless state of samadhi and witness the coming of God. I had the expectations of a light, showing up behind my closed eyes, but it never came. Instead, my heart went through random convulsions—jumping, kicking, screaming like a child throwing a tantrum. I was scared but remained peaceful. This process went on for a few minutes and then subsided. I guess it wasn't my time. When Denise and Nathan came home from Picasso's, they brought me a mini pizza, and I ate it gratefully, saying nothing about what had happened. I could not let them know.

12

THE PRODIGAL SON RETURNS

Faith is the bird that feels the light when the dawn is still dark.

~ Rabindranath Tagore

"You won't make it past my birthday—October fourth!" I sat quietly in the magnesium bath, and pondered Wayne's words briefly.

My mind ran to the calendar. "What day was it today?" I switched over from BlackBerry messenger to the calendar app, and saw it was Friday, September 21, 2012. That only gave me 10 days.

"You just need a little help," he continued, "You can't do it alone!"

I sat for a few more moments, deliberating my predicament and what I should do. In the end, "If I really couldn't do it on my own, was there really a choice?" There was just one thing I needed to know, and I typed it into the messenger app window. "Can they fix it?"

Not even a second went by before the reply came, "Yes," as if he'd been sitting there waiting for me to ask. I'd had another sleepless night, and woke up, again, with my back really tight, putting pressure on my heart. That's why I was in the magnesium bath; I woke up and prepared one right away, while Denise slept unaware. With my ringer off, it was quite fortuitous that I picked up my cell phone, just as his message came in. Wayne had tried to get me to come back to Canada and see the transplant team before, to no avail, but for some reason today I was listening. Besides, I knew I was getting information straight from his guides—that made a big difference! They also said I was strong enough to survive the flight home.

Something inside me was telling me it was time to go, but I still didn't want to admit it. I finished up in the bathroom and sat on the bed. Denise was awake now. She looked at me and asked what was wrong. I looked at her, dejectedly, and said, "Wayne said if I don't go back and get some help, I won't make it past his birthday, October fourth." She looked at me without speaking, but her eyes were entreating me to listen to him. "What will you do?" She asked.

"I think I need to go," I replied broken-heartedly. Denise knew how badly I wanted to do this on my own, and now that I was giving in, had to be disheartened. So, she reached out and held me. Deep emotions welled up, then burst forth in a shower of tears. We sobbed together for a few moments, before the pragmatic Kirk emerged and asked if she thought we could leave today. Denise was quick to act and grabbed her laptop to look at *Copa Airlines'* flight timetables online. As luck would have it, there was a flight available that day, leaving at 6:50 PM. There was also a flight on the Saturday, as well as the Monday, but I told Denise, "If it's possible, we need to leave today."

Why was I having this change of heart? Had I given up on my beliefs? I wanted to heal myself, so badly. I wanted to swim in the ocean of omnipresence and be free. I was growing tired of this life, yet did not want to return and start again, in another—reincarnation was not an option. I wanted it all, so bad, that if I couldn't have it through achieving the breathless state and meditative evolution, then I would receive it through life's attrition—death. In the morning's chat, however, Wayne made a very good point. "It's a great achievement if you can evolve while still in your body, but there's no achievement if you die in the process—anyone can do that!" That was a real, *epiphany moment*, and he was absolutely right; anyone could gain the kingdom of heaven through death—evolved, or unevolved. What I was working toward *had to* be achieved while still in the body. I had lost sight of that. Hopefully there was still time.

As we began to scramble, to pack, find a place for Nathan to stay, and prepare the place to be gone for who knows how long, I realized I better let the hospital know I was coming. There was no direct line to Stella Kozuszko, my transplant coordinator, or any of the doctors, so a message on *Easy Call* (the TGH patient messaging service) was the best I could do.

That seemed to do the trick, because in less than an hour the phone was ringing and Stella was on the line. In my Easy Call message, I mentioned that I had a rapid resting heart rate. Right away, Stella was asking me how fast, and for how long. I answered all the questions—she was willing to ask, that is! I sensed she was biting her lip, as she realized any chastising (I would or should receive) wouldn't help the situation, in any way. I got the message, loud and clear! She was also very concerned about the flight, specifically, the pressurizing and depressurizing of the plane for someone who, could potentially, be in tachycardia. She was pushing for me to be seen by a cardiologist in Panama. I might have done so, but after hearing Panamanian cardiologists may not allow me to fly home in my condition, it made my decision very easy. I needed to be with *my* transplant team, who were aware of my history, and would give me the highest chance of survival.

"The flight home…Hmmm…Never really gave that much thought" At least, not the way Stella was describing it. The flights I had taken so far, back and forth between Canada and Panama, had always been problematic. In all honesty, in the back of my mind, while on the slippery slope of late, I was always calculating that if I needed to go home to the hospital, it couldn't be at the last minute. I had to allow for sufficient strength for *the flight*. Now there was a real threat to the already-problematic airplane flights. The only consolation was that Wayne's guides told me I was strong enough to make it. That would be enough for me.

Denise had already spoken to Nathan about the need to catch a flight that day, and the urgency of my health situation. She came back to me and said, "You should have a chat with Nathan. He says he never knew you had a heart problem at all. He always thought it was your back." I immediately went to his room and sat down with him. Knowing full well there was a possibility I may never see him again, all I could do was assure him I was just going for some help, would get fixed up, and be back on my feet in no time. Then, we could get out and do some fun things together. I knew that's what he wanted to hear. Still, Nathan was very intuitive, and I could see when I looked in his eyes, he knew there was more at stake. Nevertheless, he remained composed, not taking on any more responsibility than was required to live in that exact moment.

"Was he in denial?" I wondered. "Or, did he somehow know it wasn't time to express fear surrounding an event that had not happened yet, or may never happen." Ah, the detachment of youth!

Before I knew it, Denise had found someone to drive us to the airport, a place for Nathan to stay (potentially for a couple of weeks), someone to take care of the dogs, and managed to get most of her own stuff packed—all in the same time it took me to pack my one suitcase. I knew I had to hurry but I just couldn't move that fast; I was a shell of the man I once was. It was necessary to work smarter, not harder, which wasn't an easy task considering I really didn't know how long I was leaving for. In the end, I resolved that this trip home would be permanent. The words "Time to come home!" echoed in my head, having been said by both Wayne and Stella that day.

Our friend Karen Saunders had arrived to take us to the airport. The car was packed, goodbyes said, and we were on the road. By now, our volley of FYI's to family, and friends, was bearing fruit. Emails, BBM's, and WhatsApp messages, were flying in on my cell phone. The only one we couldn't get a hold of was my mother—whom we speculated was at the casino. Not to worry, my sister Donna had been contacted, she was the true organizer in the family, and would get everyone, and everything, ready for our arrival.

Jason and Rich were shocked to hear the news. Rich especially, given that he had just been to Panama for a visit a few weeks ago and had no idea of the severity of my condition. Before I could even decline, knowing we were still financially strapped, he had already begun wiring funds to my bank account to help with the transition home. Bless his heart! What would we have ever done without his financial assistance? If there were any doubt that God was looking after me, I needed but only open my eyes to see that everything was in Divine order. I fully believe he was sent to help me, and as God is my witness, in time, I will return the favor.

My heart was like a *ticking time bomb*, and no one could hear the ticking, but me. Sometimes, the ticking would be properly paced, tick-tick, tick-tick, but sometimes it would be accelerated, tick-tick-tick-tick. I was so tuned-in to my body, I sensed every, tiny nuance of my heart. During the drive, Denise would ask me how I was doing, and the answer would always be the same: "I'm okay," no matter what was really going on. I couldn't afford to panic her. In that moment, I wish I could have made time stand still. It was about 2:30 p.m., and I knew I had to survive until almost midnight, and that would include *the flight*. It was like a long swim you had to make underwater. You had to hold your breath the entire way, and even when you realized you were only halfway but were already running out of breath, you knew that opening your mouth, and taking in water, was simply not an option. You had to fight, and endure, at all cost, as the only alternative was death.

We arrived at the airport with plenty of time to spare, bid farewell to Karen, checked in our luggage, made our way through security, and down through the hallways to the waiting area. As I sat there, my gaze dropped down to my T-shirt that was now visibly bouncing whilst it obscured the ticking time bomb inside, tick-tick, tick-tick. I casually glanced around to see if anyone could notice. No one was watching. This routine of checking to see if anybody was watching continued for some time. I was becoming very self-conscious about my condition, and whether it would be ferreted out before boarding. Remember, this was Panama, and there were always manifold, officious-looking people walking around. They were, most likely, administrative personnel making sure things ran smoothly, or security types looking for suspicious activities and/or people; they were not on the lookout for bouncing chests. Like I said, this was Panama, so who knew.

Eventually, we boarded without incident, made our way to our seats, stowed our carry-on articles, and finally, took a sigh of relief. First leg of the marathon down—we got to the airport and on the plane. Now for the second leg—*the flight*! Donna was considering having an ambulance waiting at the airport, upon our arrival in Toronto. A part of me thought, "Not a bad idea," but the stoic, macho-bravado part of me didn't think it would be necessary. Or should I say, I didn't want it to be necessary. I sat back in my seat and tried to relax. I closed my eyes and focused on the third eye center, praying, "Just get me there…five hours… Just get me there!"

Soon, we were taxiing down the runway, in preparation for takeoff. Intuitively, I felt the biggest problems would occur primarily at takeoff and while gaining altitude, then again when reducing altitude and landing. I closed my eyes again, to practice pranayama, relax myself, and find the calm center. I stayed in this space during takeoff and as we climbed to our maximum cruising altitude. It worked for the most part, except that along with the peace and calm of that sacred space was the ever-ticking time bomb. Tick-tick, tick-tick, tick-tick-tick-tick, tick…tock, tick… tock! My heart went through a myriad of ticking combinations, and a few times, there was even complete silence—rather disturbing! I remembered that my heart was denervated (the nerves were not reconnected during transplant) and could stop without warning or pain. That was the scariest part—simply fading out of existence!

My mind kept playing these mini-movie scenarios. They all seemed to involve me passing out, and/or dying, and Denise screaming for someone to revive me, or to call out for help. There was the all too predictable, "Is there a doctor on the plane?" I pictured myself lying prostrate in the aisle. I wondered if there was a special compartment where a sick person could go, and whether they could lay flat if necessary. "Would they be forced to make an emergency landing?" Imagine the shit I'd get into for that blooper! I imagined myself lying there and everybody staring at me. As I played these negative images in my mind, I could feel myself starting to tense up. Time for the magic orange ball—a hockey ball. I placed it, strategically, behind my back, leaned and relaxed against it. It put pressure on the spasm behind my left rhomboid and settled it down. Did the trick every time.

Once we got to cruising altitude, everything seemed to calm down. Sitting there, on the plane, was no different than sitting on the back porch of the casa in Coronado. I had survived many a day there and should be able to do so here, without incident. Denise was constantly checking in with me, to see if I was okay. I could see the worry and fear in her eyes. She no longer believed me when I told her I was okay…She was probably right.

In my mind, a Copa Airlines flight can be broken down into its constituent parts: the drink, the movie, the meal, the cleanup, the coffee and/or tea, and the final cleanup. Aside from the movie, you had to be aware of the gaps between the parts, in case you wanted to go to the washroom. If you got up at the wrong time, you could get stuck behind the all-pervasive, aisle-blocking, stainless-steel, serving truck. Then you'd have to wait, as it and its attendant did its duty and slowly advanced until it revealed the opening to your seat. Normally, the washroom break was the reason for breaking down the parts. This time, the parts represented phases, in the manner of a countdown. The movie was the largest, and most important phase, since you could—hopefully—get lost in the storyline and lose track of time. No such luck. I was inexorably tuned-in to the time bomb and seconds seemed like minutes, and the minutes seemed like hours, on a plane bound for destiny.

With the last flight phase complete, we were beginning our descent to the Toronto Pearson International Airport. I resumed my quasi-meditative posture, which seemed to work fairly well for the ascent. I say quasi-meditative posture because it was more like *holding my breath* for the duration of the descent, than any form of meditation I've known. This time, I threw in an affirmation: "I am the infinite that has become the body, the body as a manifestation of spirit is the ever-perfect, ever-youthful spirit", and repeated it continuously, until we landed. Did I say we landed? Thank God! In the words of my august friend, Willie Pierre, "I am blessed and highly favored!"

As we disembarked, knowing about the long hallway we would have to suffer, Denise noticed another woman waiting for a wheelchair. She asked an attendant if we could get one as well. The attendant told us she would radio ahead and see if there was one available and where we should go to meet her. As we walked to the prearranged location, we saw the attendant was standing beside a motorized passenger cart. She motioned that we come forward to catch a ride. What a bonus! We motored past all the other passengers, who were both walking and using the motorized walkways that extended the length of the very long corridor. As we rode past, I speculated as to what the other passengers might be thinking, "How does *he* rate?" or "What's wrong with *him*?" Clearly this vehicle was for passengers who were not ambulatory. Outwardly, I looked perfectly fine. The story of my life.

We were let off at the top of the escalator that led to the customs check. As Canadians with nothing to declare, we strolled through easily; then, down the escalator to the baggage claim area. Almost there…I located the nearest bench to rest while Denise reclaimed our luggage. All pieces present and accounted for. Now, we just had to hand in our customs declaration cards, then on through the big, opaque-glass, sliding-door finish line. Made it! Alive and still kicking—but barely!

As we crossed the finish line, my eyes scanned the crowd to see who was there to receive us. To my surprise, I spotted Paula and her husband, Tony Young (aka Master T[vi])…and Donna… and Allison making her way inside from the automobile pickup area—they were all there, all my siblings. They were all glowing with smiles and looks of joyous relief. As I dragged my suitcases, as well as my sorry ass, toward them, I could feel the emotion building inside me. As I hugged the first person I came to, can't even remember who that was, I broke down and let the floodgates open. What was I crying about? Was it that I made it back, against the odds? Was it the fact that I could exhale after holding my breath for so long? Or was it the fact that all my sisters, and their spouses, were there to receive me at, what had to be, almost 1 a.m.? Who knows, maybe all of them combined. One thing is for sure. It wasn't that the time bomb had been defused. Tick-tick, tick-tick, tick-tick…

The love and joy I felt emanating from my family were such that I'd never felt before. Of course, I had always known they loved me, but somehow, this was different. Was it because they came to my rescue? Had their love for me changed in some way? Or was it something in me that changed? Was it possible that I was now capable of recognizing and receiving more love? At that moment, I didn't bother to figure it out—I just let it in!

"Time to stay home now, the journey is over!" This statement was repeated, time and time again. Also repeated was, "You look good," and "You'd never know anything was wrong with you." While I know the benefits of my yoga practice helped me to keep a youthful appearance—even under great stress—I was unsure whether the words truly reflected my appearance, or whether they were intended to buoy my spirits? I may have looked healthful; however, it must have been obvious by my gait that I was in a very weakened state. Everyone helped with the luggage and we headed out to the pickup area.

13

CROSS-EXAMINATION

Until the lion learns how to write, every story will glorify the hunter.

~ African proverb

"I guess you're wondering why I didn't come home sooner," I began. "I wasn't just being stubborn you know…"

Allison's husband, Carl, was waiting in their SUV, and it was decided I would travel to the hospital with them, while the others followed. During the drive, I thought it was a good time to clarify my position: why I waited so long to save my own life.

I continued, saying, "What you'd call obstinance, I'd call strong willpower. Not really that different, except obstinance is viewed as something negative, whereas willpower, something positive. I was tired of being poked and prodded, and diced and drugged, and playing the pawn in the hospital game, but that wasn't really why I didn't want to return. It was my love for God. My Kriya yoga practice was the new foundation of my life. It was no longer *just* what I believed in, it's what I had *become*. My faith was so strong, I simply refused to consider any other means of healing my body, other than with universal life force."

"Okay, I get the poking and prodding part," Allison said. "But if you really believed you could heal yourself, then why did you come back—to medicine?"

"Divine willpower!" I replied. "When you can attune your little human will with that of God's will, you get Divine willpower. With my own will synced up with God's will, I could've healed myself—easily! Unfortunately, to get to the place where I could heal my body from any ailment, I'd need more years of practice and self-realization. Yes, I was devoutly practicing the highest methods of evolution—twice daily—but I fell a little short on the *time* factor. You could either say, I ran out of time, or I had not yet put in enough time."

"When did you know you hadn't put in enough time?" Allison asked.

I chuckled, "I guess that's where a teeny-weenie case could be made regarding obstinance. Not very long! The earliest might have been during my last trip back to Canada from Panama, and more specifically, during the return trip back to Panama. I was beginning to feel the rate of deterioration was outpacing the rate of healing. Still, in my mind, I never felt that obstinance was why I didn't return then, more like surrendering to the process. Sometimes, when we feel we have gone as far as we possibly can, and the only thing left is to lie down and let go, that's when miraculous healings can take place. Sometimes we have to go to the precipice of extinction to show that we truly believe what we say we believe. That's when we receive God's gift."

In reality, did I take it to the precipice, or did I take the coward's way out—backing down because extinction was only ten days away? I will never know. What I do know is, God also created medicine and that is something I seemed to have forgotten. Perhaps I wasn't backing down at all, but embracing what had, indeed, been given.

The reasons why I did not return sooner became somewhat of a *mantra*, because of how many times I'd have to give the same explanation. In this instance, it was in the car with Allison and Carl, the parents of (now) five children. I knew that although I had spoken about metaphysical things in the past, they would either understand my reasons for waiting so long, or they would perceive my surrendering as *allowing* myself to die. One must always accept persecutions when striving for something higher. I accepted they might think that. Sometimes people can't understand the kind of devotion I'm talking about. Don't get me wrong, I loved my family and would give my life for them—in an instant. Yet, I realized the path I must walk in this life must be my own.

It was the love that was shown to me that caused me to change my plan—my wife, my children, my family, my friends—love was coming to me from every direction, and this was just the beginning. Maybe this was God's reply? Maybe this outpouring of love was pushing me to look at things differently? Maybe my plan was not in tune with God's plan, so he sent love to awaken inside me. Maybe?

When we arrived at the emergency department of TGH, the ticking of the time bomb was barely audible. Not good. I thankfully recognized if the bomb were to go off, there were plenty of trained professionals to put the pieces all back together. Last phase complete…almost! I had to get past the first line of defense—the admitting crew. You'd think in the greater Toronto area of almost 6 million people, in a major metropolitan hospital, that there'd be hordes of people waiting to see a doctor—but the waiting room was empty. We were the only ones there. In fact, there wasn't even an admitting nurse, just a clipboard for you to put your name on and what your ailment was. Eventually, a nurse made it out to the desk and called me, to take my details.

Returning to Canada, and to the hospital, was a very big step; one I couldn't take without immediately making some adjustments to my outlook on life. I'd been through this all before. I knew what to expect when they'd call me and I'd have to pass behind those doors: I'd be here for days, if not weeks, getting sorted out. There's two ways I could do this: one, be a *total bitch* and complain about every possible thing; or two, *surrender to the medical process*, and try to be as kind and affable as possible. Intuiting this intervention to be a healing gift from above, I decided on option two—it was the only way I would survive it. Speaking of surviving, a second nurse called to say they had a room for me. Only Denise and I were allowed to go in; so, in we went.

We were taken to a room with three walls, and where the fourth wall should have been, there was a curtain separating the room and the nurses' station. I'd been in many emergency departments in my life, but this room was upscale. Normally, you'd get a stall with one wall and three curtains: two separating you from two other patients and the last one, from the nurse's station. A blonde-haired nurse, in her late 40s with a Baltic accent, entered the room. She began asking me the same questions the admitting nurse had asked but focused more on my medications and whether I had been taking them, conscientiously, while away in Panama. I knew the lay of the land in hospitals and gave her a truncated version of the truth that would explain my condition, but not get me into too much trouble. The entire process, from the body-surfing injury, to the palpitations, to the increased heart rate, was a period in excess of one year. During that time, I had dropped all my blood pressure meds and stopped my antirejection meds, completely, for at least six months. I boiled that all down to a period of three months, copped to stopping the blood pressure meds but not the antirejection meds, stating that I reduced the dosage a little, that was all. She wasn't having it! Not sure if it was just me, or what she had for dinner, but this woman wasn't having a good day. Her tone and her words were, in short, mean and nasty. "Did you ever think it's because you stopped taking your medication why your heart is rejecting?" she accused. I remained calm. First, no one had concluded my heart was rejecting. Secondly, I made a pact with myself to be kind, and so I was. I responded to her queries in a kind and loving fashion. Somehow, it worked. She left the room and came back with a gown for me to put on but somehow her demeanor had changed. I guess there was some confusion; she thought I said I had stopped my antirejection meds but when she realized it was just my blood pressure meds, and that I had stopped them because I was feeling washed out, she changed her tune. Somehow,

I knew it wasn't only the miscommunication that caused her to change. In the past, if she had been nasty to me, I would have been nasty right back. Then, on top of feeling crappy about my poor health, I'd have gotten the added benefit of feeling crappy about a negative interaction with another human being. I'm glad I decided to change. Someone had to be first. She pulled out the supplies to start an IV, slid that in painlessly, and left the room.

Denise, on the other hand, was wondering what was going on. She wondered why I had changed the history of events. I pulled her close to me and whispered, "Don't ever tell them the real story. Three months, that's how long it went on for. You never know how you may be treated if they feel like you're not playing by the rules." Then, I went on to remind her about when I received the heart transplant; how it was explained to me it was a *privilege* and not a *right* to receive a donor organ—cadaveric or otherwise. She understood, and that was always the story being told when anyone asked.

It was the wee hours of the morning. Now that I was settled in a room, the rest of the family came in to check on me and say their goodbyes. In fact, my curtain soon became a revolving door as it seemed every doctor from every discipline came in to *take a kick at the cat*. First, it was the emergency doctor, then the doctor from cardiology, then a doctor from nephrology, and so on, each time ratcheting up the hierarchy until finally I began to see transplant doctors: one from heart and one from kidney. On top of that, as the shifts were changing, so were the doctors from each category. It made me reticent to want to take the advice of any of them, individually, because as soon as the next doctor came, the advice was slightly different. I reminded myself I was surrendering to the process and left myself at the mercy of this allopathic circus.

Since it was the weekend, I fully expected a slow and pains-taking endurance in the ER. Having *lived* in hospitals previously, this was very reminiscent, and I thought that nothing significant would happen; I'd be stuck in the ER until Monday. Fortunately, with the heart transplant team now involved, word got around to me that Dr. Ross was in charge of the Transplant Step-Down Unit for the weekend. She was working on getting me a room. By Saturday afternoon, it was so.

It's amazing the social technology that's been developed in the last 12 years since my heart transplant. Between email, Blackberry messenger, WhatsApp messenger, Facebook, and text, staying in contact with numerous people, in different countries, was much simpler than before; all, right from your mobile smart phone. Even the hospital offered free Wi-Fi; a huge bonus because we hadn't had a chance to get Canadian sim cards for our phones. So far, the only person we hadn't been able to reach was Travis, but it wouldn't remain that way for long. Travis was now living in Toronto but had just gone home to his mom's place in Kitchener for the weekend. He was pretty broken up by the news, especially the fact that he was now in Kitchener when he needed to be back in Toronto. Seems he had just gotten into weekend party mode when the word hit, and he was simultaneously communicating with myself and Denise. Denise informed me he was in quite a state, was getting belligerent with her, which was unlike him, and that I should reach out to him as soon as possible.

Since there was no phone in my room, we communicated through the Facebook messaging system as follows:

September 22, 2012

1:24pm - Travis Johnson

i cant stop crying. are you okay? i just left toronto. I'm freaking out. please tell me you're okay. I'm losing it.

2:23pm – Kirk Johnson

Hi Travis, sorry you received this news so abruptly. I have been battling some serious medical conditions for over a year now. You know me, and what I believe in and have been using alternative means to heal something that is perhaps to remain only in the realm of doctors - heart transplant and all. So I had to realize that God created doctors too and they are a part of my tools for healing. Denise and others saw that I couldn't cross this last hurdle alone and so we made the decision to get help. I was getting weak, so timing was critical - plus the risk of flying in that condition. The good thing is, I survived the flight and the trip to TGH, and through the night I have received significant treatment and feel better today. I have quite a few more (invasive) tests to do to rule out all the negatives but the outlook is good. I think you may have read Denise's email as though it was a finality, but I am fighting back. Now that I have made the decision to receive this help, I am availing myself of all the services. Of course, with a heart transplant, this type of thing is serious but remember it is "will power" that determines the outcome.

When you say you just left Toronto, does that mean you are back in Kitchener?

2:49pm – Travis Johnson

you fucker... lol i knew shit was wrong last time but big kirk johnson likes to be big kirk johnson. i get it but fuck you for making me cry for hours. I've already had to live through "losing" you and i refuse to do that. i cried for too many hours, my mom was losing it, jeff was losing it. fucking talk to me. if shit is wrong then we need to fix it, just as much as my problems. fuck, fuck, fuck I'll say fuck as many times as i want, fuck (cuz im of age) fuck. you aren't invincible. i love you. but pride ain't shit. i love who you are, denise loves you, me and nathan will die without you, my mom was losing it thinking shit was wrong with you. grandma joy, paula, t, kalif, kyral, donna, kurt, tarin, ali, carl, the whole bunch, my brother dallas (who tells everyone he's Jamaican) they would be all heart broken, which is how i felt an hour ago.

2:50pm – Travis Johnson

yeah I'm messed up but get yourself together. i cant lose you. that is the most upsetting thing i could ever think of.

3:37pm – Kirk Johnson

I love you son...as well as all the others on that list. You have a life to manage and I have mine. I have done what I feel best to understand and prolong my life - including protecting those I love from repeated bad news about health. I have always had high hopes for my own health even when others didn't like the way I chose. I have never laid down on the job. In fact, I face it coura- geously every day. I have quit drugs, booze, coffee (stimulants), everything to support my health. I have made all the sacrifices.

Not out of desire to be a big man, but for you!

I am not afraid of death so could leave any time. This fight is for you and all on that list. We must all walk the path alone. You cannot judge me without judging yourself. And so it is.

Love Dad

I had never seen Travis react that way before. I cut through all the swearing and the gibberish to the heart of what he was saying. The message was coming through loud and clear; my life was important to him, my family, friends, and many others that surround me. And while I felt that my life has a purpose—one that might only have value to me as an individualized spirit— there was another purpose: to raise up, teach, inspire, care for, and love the people I'm connected to in this life. Furthermore, those people have an expectation that they'll get the chance to receive those benefits during a long life—and they have full intentions of cashing in.

As I suspected, the next day Travis had changed his tune:

September 24, 2012

1:28am – Travis Johnson

I'm sorry, I was drunk and very emotional. I just love you so much

9:38am – Kirk Johnson

I had a feeling...but its okay. This is not something small, but I will make it. I love you too and will be around to get your life rolling smoothly. I have been in all the same places and I know the way out.

Love you too, Dad.

11:30am – Travis Johnson

I will. I'm coming later around 7pm. I'll make things right

9:43pm – Travis Johnson

Are you okay?? I'm in Toronto now. I'm being strong but I need to hear from you

10:57pm – Kirk Johnson

I am ok. Just running some meds through intravenous and trying to have a nap. Looking forward to seeing you tomorrow. Hopefully it will be a brighter day.

Love you Son. Do not worry. Send me positive vibes for healing.

11:05pm – Travis Johnson

Best message I've ever read. I love you so much. I'm with Jeff *[Travis's best friend, like an adopted son]* and he loves you too. Nothing but positive vibes.

Between the ER and now in the Transplant Step-Down Unit, I subjected myself to the various procedures: X-rays of my chest and cervical spine, electrocardiograms, and echocardiograms. Regarding medications, the focus seemed to be on getting rid of the excess fluid that was onboard. We played around with various doses of Lasix to optimize fluid removal to benefit the heart, but not so much that I got dehydrated or damaged my kidney graft. That was the problem with having a transplanted heart and a transplanted kidney; one organ wanted one thing while the other one didn't, and vice versa. It was a balancing act. Unfortunately, each doctor from each discipline was a proponent of one side of the equation; the diagnosis tug-of-war was never-ending.

Eventually, this hot-potato treatment came to an end as my heart transplant team took the lead. After the barrage of tests were reviewed, it had been decided the best course of action would be to treat for the worst-case scenario—rejection of my transplanted heart. This would involve hammering my immune system with heavy-duty antirejection drugs. The best place to do that would be the Cardiac Intensive Care Unit. Tuesday morning, I checked out of the Step-Down Unit, and took up residence in the CICU.

14

TIME TO CHOOSE

If the concept of God has any validity or any use, it can only be to make us larger, freer, and more loving.

~ James Baldwin

Down in the CICU was where the real fun began. TGH was a teaching hospital, so quite often your caregiver worked closely with an apprentice. Most of the time, the caregiver, being a nurse or a tech, performed the procedure and the students watched. But sometimes...they let the student take the lead. Of course, you could refuse having the neophyte perform your procedure, but remember...I was surrendering, right? I couldn't begin to tell you how many times I'd received *extra pokes* in the name of progress. No, I'm not knocking the students. Sometimes, those students graduated to become doctors and nurses, and while still a bit green in the early days, they made mistakes too.

Case in point: I needed a central venous line inserted, to be able to handle the potent drugs I was going to be receiving. This cardiac doctor, clearly a newbie, wanted to insert the line into my neck. I gave him some of my medical history. "The pathways on the right side of my neck are occluded from repeated insertions of catheters for kidney dialysis. Also, my left side is difficult to navigate because it makes a candy-cane turn, which stops straight catheters from going in." I further told him, "I've seen scans of this pathway, so I know it's a problem." He nodded, as if he understood, but proceeded to attempt the insertion in the left side anyway. I can tell you that, even when there's freezing, this is not a pleasant experience. He poked and went in, unsuccessfully the first time, then asked if he could try again. Of course (foolheartedly), I agreed.

He went in the second time, and came back with the strangest response. "It seems to go in okay…but then it gets jammed and can't go any further." Pause…Wait for it…

"Well, duh!" Sometimes, it felt like you were on *Candid Camera.* You expected the host, Allen Funt, to jump out from behind the curtain at any second, because that's the only way this situation could have come about. I remained silent about what had just happened.

Sadly, he really needed to insert this line. I told him, "Sometimes they're able to get in *subclavian*, near the collarbone." He nodded again, in approval, then attempted that route, to no avail. While he was doing this, I could see where he attempted the insertion was not the same location I'd seen others find success in the past. Once again, I kept my mouth shut but thought, "Fail! Three pokes down—now what?" The only choice left was *the groin,* or femoral line. That was the easiest insertion, but it wasn't the best choice due to the possible complications from bleeding or clotting, not to mention the time needed to close the wound.

I was not impressed, especially since I knew I was going to need a heart biopsy within the next few days. Dr. Daley, the only doctor who I knew of who was capable of maneuvering the *candy-cane pass* uneventfully, would most likely be performing my biopsy and usually went in on the left side of the neck. Now that the left side was severely butchered after two failed pokes, the only silver lining was if Dr. Daley could be persuaded to use this femoral line that was about to be put in. The cardiac doctor agreed Dr. Daley might go for it, then proceeded to insert the femoral line. I had no qualms as to whether he'd get the femoral line in because, in terms of level of difficulty, with the proper training, even a blind man could pop that in. At this point, I'd like to add in my defense that I didn't completely dislike the medical establishment. It might seem like I was always knocking them down, but I'd played guinea pig, voluntarily, for many years in the name of medical advancement or *new lifesaving techniques.* This time was no different—I'd simply allowed, and allowed, and allowed, ad nauseum. I had done my part.

What happened next, I couldn't totally recall the order of operations. I was hooked up to some heavy-duty doses of pretty nasty drugs: an anti-inflammatory corticosteroid called *Solu-Medrol,* and—believe it or not—a product that contained antibodies derived from *rabbits,* used against T-cells in the treatment of acute organ rejection, called Thymoglobulin. At the same time, a process of diuresis had been undertaken to help remove the excess fluid. My heart, in its weakened state, wasn't strong enough to push the fluids out through my kidney. Denise was by my side, watching, as bag after bag of medications were loaded onto two poles, one on each side of my bed. There were at least 10 bags, in total. She looked down at me with tears in her eyes, and whispered, "Now I understand why you didn't want to come back." She bore witness to the pokings, and the bruising, and the bandaging that now covered those errors, and now the drug onslaught—one of which, the nurse prepared while donning a protective gown, gloves, and facemask. I looked up at Denise and her sullen, weeping countenance. I could see she was trying to be strong for me, but she had never seen anything like this during her time on this earth and the experience was wearing her down. During this hellish nightmare, she never left my side... And it was a good thing...

The solar plexus was where I normally experienced the heavy pressure from fluid buildup. The pressure made it hard to breathe. Internally, it felt like my heart was beating forcefully from inside the plexus whenever this occurred. By now, I was accustomed to this pressure; it came and went without incident—except *this time*! I felt the pressure building, and where it would normally hit a crescendo, it continued to build. Something was wrong! I voiced this concern to Denise. Normally, there were always two or three attendants by my bedside, but at this moment, there were none. Denise called out for help, and as she did so, I tried to sit up in a panicked and desperate attempt to relieve the pressure. That was a mistake…Lights out!

In hindsight, *lights out* was somewhat of a misnomer because, all of a sudden, it was *lights everywhere*! There was no longer any pressure coming from my solar plexus; there was no longer any pain at all! In fact, I no longer had a body, and it was no longer in a bed, Denise was no longer beside me, and I was no longer in the hospital. There was no longer anything…except the light… and my consciousness. "Where was I?" I was fully aware, in that moment, and cognizant of being Kirk, yet nothing remained of the physical manifestation that was Kirk. There was absolutely no audible sound. I was in an extraordinarily peaceful place, away from the din of life's sonata—no longer required to be the reluctant performer in a melodrama that was not of my choosing. The peace and serenity were very soothing, I wished "I could stay here forever!" However, on this earthly plane, such things are not meant to last. Within moments, the white light began to take on shades of gray. Soon, I was able to scarcely distinguish people who looked as though they were seated along the long aisleway of a bus, or alongside a long dining table. The perspective from which I viewed this scene was as if I were at the front of the bus or the head of the table. More and more things came into focus and the long dining table morphed and transmuted into my hospital bed, and the people surrounding it were the doctors and nurses who had rushed to my attention. I could barely make it out, but I heard someone say to inject a drug into my IV line. A few moments later, as if they thought that the first drug didn't work, I could hear them suggesting a new drug. Meanwhile, as the first drug was being injected, the double vision I was experiencing was beginning to reconnect, it slowly phased into single vision and I was beginning to see everyone and everything more clearly.

I tried to call out, to tell them that the first drug was working, but my voice box had not yet been, etherically, reconnected and the words remained as thoughts, in my mind only.

"I'm back. Crap!" I made a conscious decision to return or, "I still have work to do and was sent back to finish it. Either way, it's not my time."

A doctor began to ask me questions. "Can you tell me your name? Do you know where you are?" Both, of which I answered correctly, without pause.

I was coming around. In all the commotion, it felt as though someone had spilled something on the bed because my legs felt wet and slippery. "I think someone spilled something. It feels wet by my legs," I offered.

My nurse responded kindly, "That's okay, we'll clean it up. Sometimes, the bladder let's go during a seizure."

"Seizure? Huh…" I thought about that for a second. "Of course, it all makes sense." As I considered this revelation in contrast to the serene and peaceful place I had just been, it made me hypothesize about the suffering and agony people feared surrounding death. I'd experienced a seizure before. When you came out of it, there was aches and pain and you were completely exhausted from tensing the entire body for a time. However, with this seizure, I felt none of that. This was different. I just experienced the second seizure in my life, with all the concomitant flailing and tension, and didn't remember a moment of it. "Was I out of my body? Gone. Evicted. Persona non grata." I theorized that whenever we saw someone die in an agonizing way, that show was only a spectacle for those who remained with the living; the person we saw suffering felt nothing and wasn't even there. They had already moved on; they felt no pain at all! Interesting…In the sagacious words of Star Wars Jedi master Yoda, "Meditate on this, I will."

"Did I die and return? Did I even have a choice?" Questions played over and over in my mind. A thought came, intuitively, and stuck in my head. It whispered to me it was the right conclusion: when I'd left Panama, it was at the behest of my family and friends and not truly my own decision, like a subtle coercion. Consequently, the choice had to be put to me, directly…This time, I made the decision to stay. It was, undeniably, *my decision!* Now, to make the best of it.

Allison had arrived for a visit when the shit hit the fan, but she was not allowed to come in. Denise was allowed to stay and witnessed the entire event. She stayed in contact with everyone, keeping them informed, even at this critical juncture. While this might have seemed dispassionate, Denise reaching out let everyone know the instant the problem arose. There was a huge benefit from this; I knew I was getting help, energetically, from many sources. Allison now joined Denise. Emerging, grief stricken and teary-eyed, from behind the partitioning curtain, she tried to speak to ask me how I was feeling; but her voice trembled and broke up, as she tried to retain her composure in this troubling time. She almost lost her only brother and the prospect of that was unbearable. They both thought they would never see me again, and although they never voiced that truth, it was written all over them. I'd had so many serious things happen to me in this lifetime, yet I was always puzzled as to why people always thought I was going to die. Was it because my teachings had taught me not to fear death? Death was only a transition, like walking from the kitchen into the living room—different surroundings, yet somehow familiar. I'd died thousands of times and been reborn, never remembering the previous life. But that's reincarnation, and not truly what I'm referring to here. I felt like I couldn't die, and I wasn't talking about the foolhardy invincibility of youth, but I knew, balls to bones, that it wasn't my time. This was one of those occasions. I had to admit the white space was pain-free, blissful, and attractive—but staying there was never an option. I had to return.

It turned out to be a bad day for Travis to see me for the first time. He was supposed to come the day before, but, somehow, that visit never materialized. When he made his entrance past the curtain, I could tell he was relieved to see me alive. Nevertheless, I saw his 23-year-old, six-foot-three frame shaking from worry, like an overloaded washing machine during the spin cycle. After what had happened that day, I did my best to reassure him that I would get better. Hopefully I pulled it off, but I was starting to notice that my voice was coming out raspy and muted, in a whisper-like fashion; that aspect I wasn't able to hide, nor could I improve. It was the telltale sign of a weakened man in poor health. The one thing that stood out for me in this exchange between myself and my son was the true, unbridled love that he held for me. I always knew he loved me, but we lived such separate lives. We always had hundreds of miles between us, so the love never seemed palpable—I can't really explain it. From that day on, I resolved to forever recognize that love truly knows no boundaries, especially the love of my son Travis.

The next couple of days went by in a blur. The seizure event weakened me significantly—as if I'd needed to go down any further. Everything that happened within that timeframe occurred in a half-dreamlike state, like when you're lucid dreaming and you can direct the dream theater, and its players, in any way you like. I passed through the biopsy in this state. I did, indeed, get Dr. Daley, and he did make his way through the candy-cane pass. Unfortunately, when I asked him if he'd use the femoral line, he declined. "Oh well! Win some, lose some." Although I was near unconscious during the procedure, I was amazed at how he was able to slip the catheter in the left side of the neck, even past the botched and bruised entry sites of the day before, and into my heart—brilliant! I was grateful because I didn't think I'd be able to withstand too much more misery. I had put myself into that trancelike, meditative state, as if I weren't even in my body. That way, I was able to allow painful procedures to take place and *not fully* have their effects register with my receptors. It worked like a charm.

I remained a few days in the CICU, for observation. It was now September 28, 2012. I was getting ready to be moved back to the Transplant Step-Down Unit. Since I no longer needed the femoral line, having had received three separate blasts of the *rabbit-stew* IV drugs, it was time to take it out. Once the line had been removed, the site needed to have direct pressure applied for a period of time. Then, after it was bandaged, you weren't allowed to move your leg for about an hour—it had to remain arrow-straight. In addition, you weren't allowed to have the head of your bed elevated more than thirty degrees. Shortly thereafter, the transport orderly arrived to take me back to Step-Down and I was taken back to the 10th floor, accompanied by my CICU nurse. I arrived in Step-Down just in time for lunch. Some people hated hospital food, but I didn't mind it, and I was hungry to boot. My tray was wheeled toward me, such that the top surface was across my bed. My new nurse came in to introduce herself and make sure I had everything I needed. She asked if I would like the head of my bed elevated in order to eat, and I agreed. As the head of the bed went up, I sensed the degree of elevation was greater than thirty degrees. I wondered, "Did this new nurse read the notes to know I just had a venous line removed? Maybe the CICU nurse forgot to mention it?" Either way, I wasn't too worried about it, I was hungry!

I opened up the plate cover to reveal what was inside: sweet and sour chicken with rice and vegetables. Sadly, it looked like it came out of a box of *Lean Cuisine,* but at this point, I didn't care. I took a forkful, chewed, and when I went to swallow, a grain of rice went down the wrong pipe—I choked and coughed! As I reached for a drink to clear my throat, I felt a warmness in my crotch. Since the tray table was extended across my bed, I struggled to see what the warmness was all about. I was finally able to roll the table aside enough to see the crotch area of my gown was soaked in blood. "Seems like I blew a gasket!" I thought, and called out to the nurse who came rushing in. Good thing I had no fear of blood because the amount that was oozing out was significant—enough to make even the most moderate hemophobe pass out. I concluded, "I guess the head of the bed elevation level matters after all!" The lousy part was I had to go back to applying pressure for a while to reclose the wound. I noticed a second nurse that came in to help, immediately saw the bed was too high, and lowered it appropriately. All I wanted to do was finish my lunch, but have you ever tried eating in an almost flat position? It took most of the pleasure out of the meal, and pleasure of late was at a premium.

Eventually, the jury came in with the verdict, "Not guilty, on one count of heart graft rejection in the first degree!" The Honorable Dr. Ross stated, "Although the biopsy showed a low grade, 1A/1R level of rejection (essentially, 'inflammation'), there's no way it could have been a more serious level at the time of admission; the treatment of Thymoglobulin and Solu-Medrol could not have brought it down that quickly." She did caution, however, that there was another type of rejection—just not enough for the guilty verdict. Dr. Ross went on to discuss the other options, now that the worst-case-scenario option was put to rest. "Based on a failed attempt to open up a blocked coronary artery back in 2010, there's a concern that you're suffering from something called CAV (cardiac allograft vasculopathy). CAV is a form of chronic rejection where the blood vessels of your transplanted heart have thickened and narrowed, making it difficult for blood to pass through. The way to confirm this is to perform an angiogram. However," Dr. Ross went on, "as a result of the treatments you've received since being admitted, your creatinine level is on the rise, suggesting renal distress. Since a contrast dye will be needed during the procedure (a dye that would cause my transplanted kidney further distress) we've decided the angiogram needs to be postponed for a few weeks, to give time for your creatinine levels to normalize, and performed later, as an outpatient." The other option they were considering was to try and manage the arrhythmias with the use of drugs. One drug she added to my daily prescription routine was a drug called amiodarone, and suggested it was effective at treating heart rhythm disorders.

Dr. Ross also mentioned she'd be eliciting the help of doctors from the Electrophysiology, or EP, department. I recalled having spoken to a couple of EP guys who came to visit me while I was still in the ER. To me, these were the *last-ditch-effort guys*, who when all else failed, would choose to go into the heart and search for areas that were misfiring, then laser them to stop, or would use electric shock to restart the heart. Neither of these two options seemed very attractive to me but I was willing to try anything to get the thumping to stop and my heart rate to finish running the marathon it had begun many months ago.

15

YOU SAY TOMATO...

We do not see things as they are, we see things as we are.

~ Talmud

"Back in Panama?" I contested. "Our work is done there! The universe has our back. We're going to be taken care of. Let's put our focus on that. I'm ready to do that, aren't you?"

Denise and I were having a difference of opinion. I'd reached out to a psychic friend in Peterborough, to see if she was able to shed any light on what was happening to us. I was also concerned about our financial position, and whether she had any advice for us. The individual I reached out to, was a talented spiritual and psychic woman from Peterborough, of Irish descent, named Fiona Newman. Fiona was great! She did a full-spread reading for us. She also did heart healing prayers, sweat lodges, and solicited healing prayers from clients in her workshops and via anonymous Facebook requests. We were very grateful.

There was a ton of material in the reading, but the part that we struggled with was:

"...I have been hearing that Denise will be going back to Panama to finish some work and details. You may have a short separation (only

in distance) for a while, and that is necessary for both of you to "fall into" the next opportunity. Your focus needs to be optimum health and connecting with spirit....hers is to do what she does and does it very well...she may even set up or make connections with people that were not in your original plan...the business plans continue and are not lost...triple the income will result from this upheaval...I have heard that over and over and over...triple is nice!"

What I heard was Denise needed to return to Panama to close things up, finish things off, but she felt our success would come through furthering her real estate endeavours, and she needed to return to pursue that more fully. We went back and forth on the issue. I started feeling sorry for myself and the fear crept in. "What will people think if I'm here in Canada and she's back in Panama—especially after surviving this ordeal? What would our families and parents think?" It was time for lunch and Denise hadn't brought one, so she headed out to pick something up.

As I lay there in the bed, first I was a little pissed, then sad, then dejected. Then, I was hyper-focused on any reasons why she'd want to return to Panama and leave me here. I knew she hated the cold weather, was no longer enamored with Peterborough, and the old house had too many memories. I knew all that. Plus, Panama had the lure of nice weather, swimming pools, walks on the beach with the dogs, and an ever-popular ex-pat community that she loved to hang with. I knew that, too. I also knew what it took to get her out of that deep depression she had been stuck in for so long. The search for real happiness, regrettably, became the obvious truth that she didn't know how to find it within herself, and *that realization* was a heavy cross to bear. Once she had finally taken a stand, found something she really liked to do and was very good at, the thought of it being taken away prematurely was like a shot in the gut.

Suddenly, as if someone had just turned on a light in a dark room, came these thoughts. "What are you thinking? You idiot! This is for you, as well as her. You know how you like your quiet time. Use this time wisely, to heal, to meditate, to pray. This is a blessing in disguise. Don't throw it away. Let it go..." Within a few moments, a calm peace came over me and I began to feel better. What had come over me? I guess that's how I used to be in the past—childish, selfish, and always looking for a way to justify my view. I was beginning to see the benefits of what the universe was proposing and was liking what I saw. I also liked the fact that I caught myself *being the old Kirk*, in a mental rant that would've eventually developed into a verbal rant and an unnecessary argument. Kudos!

When Denise returned with her lunch, she looked at me, dejectedly, and said, "You're right. I need to be here for you. We can't afford both places anyway. I just need to go back, pack up, and get back here as soon as I can."

I looked into her eyes and said, "No, you are right. You worked hard to get to where you are now. Now is not the time to let it go. We will work it out. And I will be fine on my own—you know me. I will use the time to heal, and meditate, and get back to the gym, and get this body back in order. You don't need to be here for that." She was so happy and grateful to hear those words, and we embraced each other. As I held her, I contemplated her unconditional love for me that she would give up what she wanted most, to see to it I was okay. Not many people would do that. Actually no, a lot of people would do it, given the circumstances, but then never let you hear the end of it. So, you'd pay for it… for life! Homey don't play dat!

We were heading into another weekend and there was no sign of the EP team. The doctor on call let us know that if we hadn't heard from them by Monday, we'd get Dr. Ross to call the head of the EP department to get the ball rolling. Nothing to be done but wait. By that time, I was able to get out of bed and make a few rounds of the hallways. Okay, maybe one or two rounds. I was still very weak and lightheaded as I walked, but from experience, I knew that this was what you had to do—get up and get going! I wasn't the only one doing that. From time to time, while I lay in my bed, I watched as newly transplanted recipients made their way through the Step-Down corridors. In namesake, that's what the Transplant Step-Down Unit was truly for—people who'd just received a transplant but were not sick enough to remain in the recovery ward. These people were still very ill, and you saw that by the facial swelling and discolorations, multiple IV meds hanging from poles, walking assistance implements, and personal assistants. These folks were a hell of a lot sicker than I was. Then again, maybe not. Appearances weren't everything.

My family was always there, too, coming and going, sometimes individually and sometimes in sync. My mother, once we wrested her away from the casino, was a frequent visitor. Her goal was to relieve Denise as much as possible. "I'm taking the night shift," was her mantra as she would normally roll in early evenings and stay late—sometimes, a little too late. Nevertheless, my mother was named Joy for a reason. I'm not sure if it was her demeanour, or her storytelling delivery, but my mother could keep anyone in stitches for hours. The simplest tales became some of the best jokes. She always brought fun and laughter, even to some of the most morbid of situations.

My sister Donna, at times accompanied by her teenage son, Tarin, had also been visiting. When she wasn't visiting, she was regularly staying in touch via text messaging. While she was home, she often received messages from *the other side*. On one occasion, it was our father who visited. He instructed Donna to tell me to *give it all to him—all the pain, and suffering, and sadness, that I had experienced in my life, give it all to him!* Knowing my father as I did, this was his gift to me in my time of need. I'm sure he'd hoped that by giving all my pain and suffering to him, I could finally let go of some of the emotional baggage that had weighed me down. From what I understood, most disembodied spirits no longer felt the delusive draw of attachment to material things; they looked back on their lives and wondered why they'd done what they'd done and felt remorse, because other people got hurt. In life, my father put himself in a position where he wasn't able to help me anymore. So, in death, as he lived in his astral body, he was freer to affect my life in a positive way than he ever was while he was alive. My first wife, Lorie, had also come to visit Donna, and instructed her to bring something to me. It was something Lorie had previously bought for Donna on her birthday: a wood carving, about the size of the baseball, that was of a man seated in lotus position, bent forward with his elbows touching in front of him, such that his forearms and hands covered his face and the top of his head. Many people who entered the room asked me why I had *a potato* on my table, until they got close enough to see what it was. As soon as I saw it, I knew what to do. Similar to what my father had offered, Lorie was offering the same, in her own way. I held *the potato* against my heart and allowed it to draw out any negative energies that remained in my heart, or anywhere else in my body. I used this tool many times during my stay.

Paula and Tony also came often, along with their sons, Kalif and Kyral. Paula was very insightful, having gone through some difficulties in her own life. She'd struggled with severe postpartum depression after the birth of both her sons. She knew what it was like to *lose yourself* and have to find your way back. Paula was also like the *video recorder* of the family—she remembered everything. She too, had a strong sense that much of this *last piece* had to do with letting go of the issues surrounding my father. We spent a great deal of time revisiting those past issues as she recounted the details—some of which were so repressed I didn't even remember. Tony was my cornerstone. He went out of his way to get whatever it was that I needed or to help in any way that he could. It was one thing to have offered, but I knew it was no small task to find free time when his family was in the midst of preparing their house for sale. Plus, he was the sole driver in the household, with two school-aged kids involved in sports. Bless his heart!

Allison's work in Toronto saw her traveling to meet with clients throughout the week. That schedule gave her the flexibility to pop in and visit from time to time. Her job was high stress, so we discussed how to make it through in one piece as well as her *next steps* in life. She was running from pillar to post as she managed a chaotic lifestyle that included being a parent of five children—with one still an infant. Her husband, Carl, was a serial entrepreneur, so for him, time was also at a premium. They were the quintessential, twenty-first-century family, with two income earners, fighting for the dream while they simultaneously managed a family of going concern. In all the kerfuffle, she still managed to sneak me some baked goods into the hospital. Thank goodness for small mercies!

Monday went by, and no EP team…Tuesday went by, and no EP team…By Wednesday, in the routine switching of doctors, somewhere, sometime, someone got the idea it was time to try more drugs to try to bring down my heart rate. The doctor was going to start me on a very low dose of 12.5 mg of metoprolol for the heart rate, and carvedilol to help strengthen my heart—can't remember the dosage. I popped the new pills with my morning *multitude,* and Denise and I went for a walk. I was feeling good this day as I made the first round, and the second. I knew I was pushing a bit to attempt the third, but you had to push—a little. The hallways were like one large block with a couple of avenues in between. On the third round, something felt a little funny; weakness and dizziness had set in. Fortunately, we were close to one of those avenues, and right at the turn was a wheelchair, sitting there. Denise suggested, "have a seat, maybe you've overdone it." I rested for a few moments. I waited long enough until I found the strength to continue along the avenue-shortcut, back to my room. Even though I'd spent nearly two weeks lying in a bed, I was grateful to get back into one. I collapsed into the bed and found it difficult to raise my arms or legs.

"What was going on?" Then it hit me. I had felt this before. Over the course of the previous years, I had many occasions that necessitated an adjustment to my blood pressure medications. In finding the optimal dose, the doctors made small increases, saw how you tolerated it, then increased again. You knew it was increased too much when you started to feel *washed out*! Washed out meant that the medication given to bring a high blood pressure down to normal, had gone past normal, and was approaching a *low blood pressure* situation. Along with that low blood pressure, came a number of unfavorable symptoms, namely: overall weakness, dizziness, fainting spells, and nausea. I was having them all—right then!

When the doctor came in, I was lying splayed across the bed with my arms and one leg hanging off the sides, like a rag doll. "What's wrong?" she asked.

I told her, "I think I'm washed out. They tried metoprolol when I first came into the ER, and it didn't go well there, either."

"Okay, I'll stop it for now," she agreed. I was relieved. I felt it was a good time to have a heart-to-heart with this doctor. I have to say, she was the one who I saw most often, and I found she had a very caring, bedside manner. She had a slender build, stood about five-foot-four, and was of Asian descent—both visibly, and with a slight accent—but I, sadly, can't remember her name.

I began by telling her, "I've had this constant, hard thumping of my heartbeat. It doesn't feel like it's going to be controlled by drugs. There's something else going on. I've been very patient while they've ruled out rejection, got the fluid overload under control, and tried to correct the rhythm with meds—and now the metoprolol isn't working."

She responded positively, as not all doctors would to a patient suggestion, and told me, "I'll push further to get the EP team here as soon as possible, so they can share their insights into your condition." I couldn't have asked for more!

16

WAITING FOR THE LATEST EP

*Faith is taking the first step even when you don't
see the whole staircase.*

~ Martin Luther King Jr.

I was constantly on the lookout for the EP *dynamic duo* and
was pretty sure I'd recognize them, having seen them while
I was in the ER. Two fairly young men, sharp looking, who
looked like they had the world by the balls—okay, yes, a little
arrogant. With that in mind, I was a little surprised when I saw a
tall, thin, gray-haired man enter the room and introduced himself
as the EP Head. He had been going over my chart and stated he
noticed some underlying irregularities in my ECGs. "Finally!" I
thought. "Someone noticed this isn't a garden-variety case that
can be controlled by drugs alone."

He went on to discuss what might be taking place. "In a
normal heart, the chambers fire an electrical impulse in sequence,
but sometimes a new spot develops that also has the ability to
fire." "In a transplanted heart," he continued, "this renegade
firing spot would usually develop along the scar tissue of the
heart graft but has been known to develop in other places, too.
What needs to be done is, with the use of a contrast dye, to run

a catheter up through the groin with a device that can map out the inside of your heart in order to find where the irregularity is originating from, and once we find it, we'll use a small laser to burn the source, and stop the misfiring. That burning process is called a *cardio ablation*."

Two things jumped out at me: groin and contrast dye! "Another groin entry—grrr!" I thought. "I could live with that, but I've already got concerns about using a contrast dye in the upcoming angiogram. Now more dye? What about my weakened kidney?" I mentioned these issues to him.

He looked at me puzzled, then asked, "When did you have a kidney transplant?"

"In 2003," I answered. He then asked if I could give him a minute to check something and he left the room.

"He didn't know I had a kidney transplant," I realized, sadly. This wasn't the first time a doctor had come in to see me, merely skimmed my chart—which was readily available outside of my room—and was ready to prescribe medications and procedures without knowing some pretty important history! I said nothing. I was just grateful to know that something was finally going to be done to end the marathon pounding in my chest. I was further grateful that my condition favored *cardio ablation* over *cardioversion*: in which they'd use an electric shock to restart the rhythm of my heart. Every time I heard about that, my mind ran to scenes in movies where, in a code blue situation, the doctor had two paddles in hand, shouted "Clear!" and then applied the paddles to the patient's chest while the patient, even though unconscious, arched his back way up in response to the electric shock. I couldn't imagine what that would feel like if you were awake. Of course, I realized that the procedure wouldn't have been that extreme. Still, not the option I wanted. When the good doctor came back, he stated that the procedure could be conducted without the use of a contrast dye.

He also said, "I don't want to rush your decision, but I can schedule the procedure for tomorrow. There's a number of others getting done then, too. I can't guarantee it, but there's a very good chance. If not, it'll have to be next week."

"Tomorrow sounds perfect to me," I quickly replied. Time to get 'er done!

The next day, I sat in my bed staring at the breakfast tray sitting on the counter. Later, it was the lunch tray sitting on the counter. I was getting hungry but wasn't allowed to eat anything since midnight the night before, in anticipation of the cardio ablation procedure. Since they were fitting me in, there was no scheduled time. I was at the mercy of the procedure times of the patients who preceded me. What really sucked, was there was no guarantee I would get in that day. The hours were ticking by and I knew if they didn't come soon, I wouldn't get in; I'd have to wait in the hospital, over the weekend, for another chance on Monday. Three p.m. is what I kept hearing, if they didn't come by 3 p.m., the chances of getting it done that day were slim to none. Fortunately for me, around 2:30 p.m., an attendant came to pick me up and took me to the prep area for the procedure.

In the prep area, I did all the usual things: spoke to the doctor who would be doing the procedure—a man of about five-foot-seven, with a slender build and black hair, who seemed to be of East Indian descent. Then I signed the waiver form that stated, essentially, if I died in the process, it wasn't their fault. The EP Study Lab was similar to the Cath Lab in terms of the equipment that was available and the way they prepped you for the procedure, except for one thing: in the EP lab, they didn't use the little, round stickies—they used *really big stickies* that got stuck to your chest and back. I assumed the purpose of these was, when connected to the monitor, that they allowed the doctor to see inside you. Although I was covered up, I saw what the doctor saw on the monitor above and to the left of me. My groin was shaved and painted with an antibacterial substance, but the nurse who was applying the liquid went a little hog-wild and nicked my genitals. "That stings like a be-otch!" I thought. "Nothing I can say, really; just grin, and bear it! Nature of the beast, I guess."

The doctor inserted a needle with some freezing into the groin area and, shortly thereafter, went in. As he slid the catheter in, I watched on the screen as he began mapping out the inside of my heart, using some kind of device that placed little round markers at various points within my heart. While I could only see him out of my peripheral vision, while I lay covered up, he looked as though he were a big kid playing a videogame. You know that look: the one where the kids are sitting on the couch, with their arms hanging down and their hands on their laps. They hold the controller and move it side to side as if the moving of it, and not the pressing of the buttons, was influencing the game in some way. Meanwhile, their heads are fixed in the direction of the screen, and their eyes are hyper focused on what they're doing—as if they were possessed. We've all seen it! Except this was a grown man and what he was controlling was no videogame.

What made it even more videogame-like, was a group of doctors, or technicians, watching, either via monitor or directly through a large glass window, and they seemed to be cheering him on. Just like when kids played, the other kids who watched got right into the game as much as the kid with the controller, enjoying the fun as they waited for their turn. What I found interesting was they communicated with the doctor performing the procedure and spoke aloud, as if I wasn't even there. They congratulated him on marking this, suggested he mark that, or suggested he move in a different direction. All of a sudden, the little symbol he controlled, to mark locations, turned a different color and a different shape, and a roar emanated from the peanut gallery. The onlookers were entreating him to go back and find that spot. From where I lay, I also knew the spot they were referring to was the spot they'd been looking to laser. He searched, and he searched, and he searched, but could not relocate that exact spot.

This went on for quite some time and he was about to give up looking for it when it appeared again. This time, he locked onto it and fired the laser, like Luke Skywalker firing on the Death Star. While I understood I wasn't supposed to feel anything, I felt a sharp tensing of the muscles that ran along the outside of my neck. The pain was so sharp, it felt like it was burning—very odd. Nevertheless, I was so elated, along with the rest of the gang, I didn't bother to say anything about it. With the first hit of the laser, my heart rate began to drop. They knew they had found the right spot. As I continued to listen to the banter, I understood that the spot they were lasering was very close to my own node—the naturally occurring part of my heart that initiates the firing sequence—and they didn't want to damage that. The doctor stopped for a moment and explained to me what was happening, as if I hadn't overheard. He needed to tell me because they were going to attempt to burn it further to ensure they knocked out the renegade firing location while leaving my native node intact. The danger was that if they burned too far, they could knock out my native node, requiring a pacemaker to be put in. "Pacemaker...Not digging that!" I reflected. While I didn't like the sound of a pacemaker in any way, shape, or form, I needed this procedure to be done completely, so I gave him the go-ahead to continue.

There was a monitor directly in front of me that displayed my vitals—blood pressure, heart rate, and others. When the doctor re-engaged the laser, I stared at the monitor display and watched as my heart rate dropped: 95...82...76...61...54...43...37... Oh shit...Not only was I able to see my heart rate dropping on the monitor, but I felt it, and internally heard it as well. The space between the beats got longer, and longer, and longer...The spaces seemed so long, I could've run out and grabbed a coffee in between. All kidding aside, it was a freaky feeling, and a little disconcerting—I was fading out! All of a sudden, there was a lot of commotion between the doctor, his assistants, and the peanut gallery. There was an appeal for somebody to artificially stimulate my heart rate. Once the scrambling subsided, my heart rate was artificially brought back up to around 77, and it settled there. The discussions continued, back and forth, wondering if they had burned too far. I was pretty concerned, too; the prophecy of the pacemaker was almost palpable now, given what was going on. Next thing I knew, someone asked if my heart rate was still being controlled artificially, and to my relief the doctor replied, "No, he's on his own now." Cheers and adulation filled the room as the doctor was being congratulated for a successful procedure. No one said anything to me this time, but I recognized the doctor's success to be my own. I glanced once again at the monitor and not only was my heart rate registering at 77 but there were many other sevens on the screen at the same time. I immediately recalled the meaning of triple seven: "The Angels applaud you… Congratulations, you're on a roll! Keep up the good work and know your wish is coming true. This is an extremely positive sign and you should also expect more miracles to occur." With a smile, I received that message loud and clear. Remember that ticking time bomb… *Time bomb defused*!

As the doctor was removing the catheter, and the assistants were adeptly tearing down the equipment, like carnies at the end of an expo, the doctor informed me of the success they'd had. "The ablation should solve most of the problems you were having." He then asked, "What medications are you on?" As I rolled through the list, he shook his head and informed me, "You'll no longer need the amiodarone, nor the carvedilol. They should be stopped, immediately."

"Bonus!" I sighed in relief to myself. Not only did I get my heart rate fixed but I also got paroled from some nasty and excessive medications. "Now there's a *twofer* for ya!" I thought as I lay back on the gurney and contemplated the great success of the day, while they wheeled me out of the EP lab, through the halls, and back to my room in the Step-Down Unit.

The EP lab team was first-rate! Three of them escorted me back to my room. They made sure that my nurse knew exactly what had taken place and left notes for the doctors regarding the procedure, as well as the medication reductions. Once again, since they had gone through the groin, I had to lay with my leg straight for an hour or so, and…make sure my bed wasn't elevated above thirty degrees. One of the doctors mentioned, "Sometimes the procedure can revert back. Usually, one hour is the litmus test; if the adjusted heart rate doesn't revert back within one hour, then it should last. He then informed me, "It's been just over an hour since the final burn, so things are looking very good." I thanked him and the other members of the team wholeheartedly—no pun intended—and they left.

Finally, the day came to check out. Unfortunately, being discharged by the hospital is nothing like leaving a hotel: all you had to do was return your room key, sign your credit card receipt for any incidentals, and you're done. Sometimes, it was even shorter than that with Web, or television check out. Not here. When you're told it's time to go you think you'll be out in no time. Not so. First, they've got to send someone down from the pharmacy to make sure you've got all the medications that you'll need to take. Then, someone has to go down and pay, of course—a small mortgage for antirejection medications that run about $1,000 a month—each! Thank God for my health plan. I was still able to participate as a *retired* public service employee. Even with 80% coverage, that left me with a $200 bill every month—no small potatoes! Then, the nurse had to come in and unhook you, and unplug you, from all the devices and IV lines you'd become accustomed to. Time to go? No, now you have to wait for them to find a doctor to write up your discharge summary—and those summaries take a good 20 to 30 minutes for them to type out. Now, finally, finished and ready to walk out the door. Whoops! The doctor forgot to sign the discharge summary, or sign me out, or something like that, and the nurse that day, who was built like a brick shit house, wasn't letting me go until she got a signature. In my frail state, I wasn't ready to go a round of Brazilian jujitsu with this woman. She would have me tapping out in no time. Finally, the doctor returned, and Denise and I were heading out, drugs in hand, with a promise to follow up with a clinic appointment the following Thursday.

Up to that point, I'd only made a few rounds of the hallways successfully, but now, I had to make the long journey out of the hospital. You sat there for days and days waiting, and hoping, to be released, and then when the time came, you realized the hospital and its many attendants was like a warm security blanket, providing instant comfort when needed. Now, it was time to leave that comfort and security behind, and the prospect of it was daunting. Anything could happen out there in the real world. It was going to take time for my body to adjust to the new programming. Leaving now was like your first few days of riding a bike—you got on with confidence and the knowledge that you'd done it before, but once you kicked off, there was always the thought in the back of your mind that you might fall. Questions and doubts arose. "Have they fixed everything? Will the ablation hold? I still feel the tightness across my chest and back. Why is that still going on? Walking around with dizziness and blurred vision, like you're stuck in a dream that won't end; how long will that last?" The ego was always telling you that you had to keep up appearances. You worried about what people thought, as you walked slowly. As you paused at times, you looked for something to grab onto while you made your way down the long corridors of the hospital. "Enough!" I'd tell myself. "You've been here before. Fake it until you make it! Keep on keeping on!"

17

PILLOW TALK

Look fear in the face and it will cease to trouble you.

~ Swami Sri Yukteswar Giri

Thump-thump…Thump-thump…Thump-thump…I woke up at 1:31 AM to the sound of my own heart beating—amplified through my pillow. In addition, my right arm, which was folded across my chest as I fell asleep, was now completely numb. So numb, it took a few minutes before I was able to move my hand or fingers—very freaky! I had never felt it this extreme before.

It took a moment to realize where I was. Since I had to stay in Toronto for a follow-up appointment and was too weak to go back and forth from Peterborough, Denise's friend, Karen Lunn, said I was welcome to stay at her place as long as I needed. In truth, there wasn't much of a decision to be made, given the status of my mother and siblings: Donna had an extra room, but it didn't have a bed in it; Paula and her family were preparing their house for sale, so a rehabilitating houseguest was not in the cards; Allison had five kids and the little ones loved the attention, so there would be little rest to be had there; and finally, my mother was promoting her place as the best place to stay, but she only had one bedroom and one bed, and while she denied sleeping on the couch, or a single mattress on the floor, was a problem, I had trouble putting her out in that way. Karen and her daughter, Ciera, would be at work and school most of the day, so it would be quiet and peaceful. Like I said, not much of a decision needed to be made.

The beating continued: thump-thump…thump-thump… thump-thump…"Is it getting faster?" Thump-thump, thump-thump, thump-thump. "I hope not!"

My mind ran back to Dr. Ross telling me, "Sometimes the ablation doesn't hold, and the tachycardia can return." Thump-thump, thump-thump, thump-thump…Panic was setting in. Thump-thump-thump-thump-thump-thump…

"Yep! It's definitely getting faster!" I felt my legs starting to tingle—with a simultaneous feeling I had to have a bowel movement; these signs were not good. Here I was again, at a crossroads. Something was happening that was definitely not good. I remembered being in Panama and always *knew* what 120 bpm felt like; I was there now, and maybe more. "I should call out to Karen for help," I speculated. "I'm going to need ambulance."

Why I didn't call out right away, I'm not sure. I closed my eyes and focused on the third eye center. Every time I did that I expected to see the white light coming for me, but it never did. Meanwhile, my fast-beating heart, which had been thumping forcefully, was still thumping rapidly, but the forcefulness was dying off…and possibly, so was I. I was okay with it. It wasn't scary at all; it felt peaceful. I lay there for a while…in that peaceful space. Then, logic kicked in: "I can't die in Karen's house—she'd never get over it…and besides, it's just not right," I thought. "It's also Denise's birthday today—I can't die on her birthday—she'd never forgive herself for returning to Panama. What about Travis, and Nathan? They would be devastated! My mom, my sisters, my friends…What the hell am I thinking? I can't die today… Ka-ren!!!!!!!!!!"

"Yes," she answered, as if she was awake, awaiting my cry.

"I think I need to go to the hospital," I bellowed back. Within moments Karen came through the door.

"Should I call an ambulance?"

"Yes," I nodded vigorously.

By the time the ambulance arrived, I was starting to take on *the shakes*. Karen did her best to explain to them my history: that I needed to get to the Toronto General Hospital as soon as possible, that my transplant team knew what to do. Strangely, to me at least, as if they hadn't heard her advice, they began to treat me like I was having a heart attack; asking me questions about pain in my chest, numbness, tingling, etc. They hooked me up to a portable monitor: heart rate was 136 bpm and blood pressure was 160/119!

Karen spoke up again and reiterated, "It's not a heart attack, he is a post-transplant patient who has recently had a cardio ablation procedure because they thought he had heart transplant rejection!" Still, they went on with their work. By this time, I was trembling so much, my heart was beating so fast—yet, so weakly—I thought it was truly the end.

Karen was at the foot of the bed. I looked up at her and said, "I think I'm going out."

She sternly repeated, "He's going out!" and in response, they quickly strapped on an oxygen mask. After I took a few deep breaths, things didn't seem so bad. Don't get me wrong, things were still desperate…just, not so dreadful. Unbelievably, the big delay was they didn't think they could get me down the two flights of stairs from the top floor and had called for backup.

"What the fuh?" I mulled. "All the houses in Toronto and they've never faced stairs before? Like, I'm dying here, and I've been sent *Ren and Stimpy* to bail me out?" All I could do was shake my head and chuckle, inwardly.

Since I appeared to respond to the oxygen, one attendant asked me, "Can you stand? Do you think you could make it down the stairs?" By this time, I didn't know if I could walk, but I was sure as heck going to try; this dog and pony show was going on for much too long. I felt that time was of the essence. They helped me up, and with their assistance, sure enough, I made it down to the main entrance hallway and then onto a stretcher.

On the way out, they made sure I had my wallet and, more particularly, my OHIP (Ontario Health Insurance Plan) card—"Cuz they gotta get paid, ya know!" Karen retrieved it from my knapsack, and we were on our way.

The male attendant was with me in the back of the ambulance as we drove to the hospital. He continued to ask me more questions: when was my heart transplant? When was my kidney transplant? He was surprised that I'd had both. Over the years, I found that sentiment to be quite common: people were surprised! What were they surprised about? That I was still alive? That I was too young to have gotten so sick? Or that, other than the desperate characteristics of the moment, I really didn't look that ill. There were other people who had *only* a heart transplant, or *only* a kidney transplant, and looked a whole lot worse. Who knew? He took my blood pressure and it had dropped down to 137/102, and my heart rate had dropped to 100. I was relieved, but, at the same time, hoped my vitals didn't normalize before I reached the hospital. Yes, I knew that would mean I was getting better, or that nothing was excessively wrong, but I would've also felt like a bloody fool arriving in an ambulance in perfectly good condition—the ultimate Catch-22. While I was in the bus I spent some time looking around the inside of the rear quarters of the ambulance. Such a common thing. You saw it on the television, and in movies, all the time: people getting picked up and hauled off to the hospital in an ambulance, but never really knew what that felt like. I did now! It was not the most comfortable ride. If you weren't strapped in, you'd end up on the floor every time the driver made a left turn. I was grateful there weren't too many of those. Before long, we pulled into the emergency ward entrance of the hospital.

After the emergency crew wheeled me in and transferred me from the gurney to a bed, a doctor from cardiology came and started me on a small dose, 12.5 mg, of metoprolol. I was a little hesitant to get on that drug again, but with recent events,

I was willing to give it another try. I popped the pill. Amazingly enough, within 20 minutes my heart rate began to fall, 100, 95, 90, 85, 80, then settled in around 77 bpm. Sweet! Funny how the same drug, at the same dose, had knocked me right out, then a few days later, was the exact thing I needed. The Lord works in mysterious ways, indeed! My blood pressure improved, coming down to 127/ 87. My thoughts ran back to the recent clinic appointment with Stella and Dr. Goldrick, after I had been discharged from the hospital, and how they planned to get me on metoprolol in the near future. I guess it wasn't near enough. Ah…The best laid plans of mice and men.

In the morning Dr. Ross arrived. As usual, she was strictly business. First off, she addressed the results of my ECG upon arriving the previous night, commenting that, "Your ECG looks a lot like the ECG you had when you first returned from Panama."

"Crap! That ain't good!" I thought to myself.

She then went on. "But it looks like the addition of metoprolol had a significant effect in resolving the issues that transpired last night. Hopefully that remains stable. We were waiting for your creatinine levels to fall in anticipation of an imperative angiogram procedure. However, the events of last night compel us to expedite the angiogram and have it done as soon as possible, while you're in hospital. We're also reconsidering the use of amiodarone to, once again, address your heart rhythm." The funny thing with Dr. Ross was that you could spend a lot of time deciding what you want, or don't want, regarding your healthcare, but as soon as she explained to you what she thought needed to be done, you just said, "Okay." I wasn't sure if it was her delivery, or her demeanor, but she walked with a powerful energy behind her. Silently, I hoped the amiodarone wouldn't be necessary. I already felt the drug had damaged my vision.

"And what's with this ECG looking like it did nearly three weeks, and a whole bevy of procedures, ago? That ain't right!" I seriously hoped I had not lost all the benefits of the cardio abla-tion. But how could I have? It was the ablation that allowed my heart rate to drop below 100. I peered up at the monitor and it smiled down at me at 78 bpm. That wasn't possible before I had the ablation; none of the drugs they tried could simulate that. I thought I'd reserve my judgment and see what happened next.

In preparation for the upcoming angiogram, I was visited by a nephrologist, Dr. Joseph Kim. He came to give me the pros and cons of the procedure, as it pertained to my kidneys. I remembered him from the days of my original heart and kidney transplants and recalled liking him then. For some reason, that made what he had to say more meaningful to me. Once again, the concern was the use of the contrast dye and the effect it would have on my kidney graft—which was already diminished in its capacity. He gave me the percentages of what might happen and there were three possible outcomes: one, that it would be *damaged beyond repair*; two, that it would be *somewhat* damaged, necessitating a number of dialysis treatments until it came back online; and three, that there would be *very little effect*, and any lack of onboard fluid removal could be handled with drugs, such as Lasix. Fortunately, the chances of the worst-case scenario were low, if not negligible, and the doctor believed the benefits of locating any problems in the coronary arteries greatly outweighed the risk to my kidney.

I immediately keyed-in to that all-too-familiar buzzword, *dialysis*. "The threat never goes away!" I thought to myself. Of course, yes, I had to go through this procedure; it was one of the last boxes to tick in a long process that was hopefully drawing to an end. Now, I had the bonus of worrying about the auspice of dialysis hanging over my head, in addition to all the other worries. "Hang in there, little kidney" I coaxed myself. "You're gonna make it!"

The day came for the procedure and I was wheeled down to the prep area. My mom and sister Donna were both there. They sat by my side while I signed the paperwork, and watched the nurses get the necessary IVs going. Then nurses ran a sodium bicarbonate drip to protect the kidney prior to, and during, the procedure. I liked the sound of that. I was introduced to the doctor who would perform the angiogram. From where I lay in the bed, he looked to be about five-foot-six, lean build, with black hair, stylish, black thick-rimmed glasses, and a fairly strong English accent; he almost had an *Elvis Costello* thing going on. Funny how we felt the need to size up the person who was going to perform something invasive in our bodies. Overall, he seemed sharp and professional enough to get the job done. Once again, they would be going in through the groin. "*Faaaaaack*! Not again!" The area was still sore from the last two or three entries. Oh well, it's the nature of the beast. Grin and bear it!

The time came to bid my sister and mother farewell, and I was wheeled into the Cath Lab. Inside the lab, there was always a number of people milling about: getting all the instruments together and covering the equipment with plastic. I noticed a young male nurse, or technician, walking around and I wondered what role he would play. What made him stand out was that, although he was pretty much covered by his gown, gloves, mask, and cap, there were a couple of large tattoos that were exposed on his neck. Now, I was no prude, and had seen many a tatt, but my mind struggled with there being a young tattooed individual in an area where I was receiving an invasive procedure. I could get past the tattoos, but every time I looked at him, he just stared back at me, then looked away like he was hiding something—weird! Perhaps I'd just watched too much TV: where the villains infiltrated the hospital and sent in the hitman, disguised as a doctor or nurse, to take you out! It felt like I was living that! Lastly, since I couldn't tell what his function was, I seriously hoped he wasn't going to be the one poking needles into my already sore and tender groin.

Thank goodness it was Elvis Costello who came in, applied the freezing, and made the first poke. Unlike the recent biopsy and cardio oblation procedures, this poke was into the artery and not the vein. Even though there was freezing, it still smarted like a *mofo*! Thank goodness I was on an intravenous line; they ran something to take the edge off. As usual, I went into that low, ebbing, meditative state to allow my body to relax from the stiff, rock-solid posture you take on when you're about to encounter pain. These procedures always go so much better when you relaxed.

Again, as I lay on the table, I looked up at the video screen and could see everything that was going on. I could see that one of the main arteries, which fed into many smaller branches, was significantly blocked. The doctor inserted a catheter that could deliver a stent into the blockage, then pushed it open. The stent, once opened, looked much like a small piece of a drinking straw. It allowed the blood to flow more freely to the constricted area. Almost immediately, I felt a sense of lightness, like the boot that was stepping down on my chest had been lifted. What a relief! Speaking of relief, during the procedure, the tattooed man asked how I was doing from time to time. It seemed as though he had something to do with the anesthetic. As it turned out, he wasn't a bad guy after all. Time to get rid of those stereotypes. They no longer serve me, nor anyone else.

The new stent and medication adjustments tuned things up nicely. After I was discharged, the bedtime, heart-thumping *pillow talk* subsided, and I enjoyed a few carefree days. This was the day I'd be heading to Peterborough. While I was a little reticent to be leaving Toronto and its easy accessibility to the hospitals, I was glad to be getting out of the big city. Although I would be a few days at Denise's parents' place, I was anxious to get back into our home and some peaceful solitude. I was also a little concerned about making the hour-and-fifteen-minute drive alone, not having driven since coming back to Canada. I quickly packed up my gear and left a small gift for Karen: a laser pointer pen she had spoken about that she could use to entertain her large, orange tabby cat, Farley. I knew she would like that.

Thank goodness Karen's house was so close to the Don Valley Parkway (DVP). My plan was to avoid too many starts and stops. Once I got on the DVP, it would be a short haul from Lawrence Avenue to Highway 401, a straight line on the 401 from Toronto to just past Bowmanville, and then North on Highway 115 all the way to Peterborough. Also, if I got tired, there was a coffee shop and other service outlets that I could stop for a rest just as I headed north on the 115. The car was tuned in to a radio station that played classical music, so I put my head back on the headrest, the car in cruise control, and started down the highway. It wasn't long before I began to notice the vibration of the tires meeting the road. I was starting to feel a little woozy, and as I did a flood of thoughts ran through my mind, "What if I pass out at the wheel? I'm in the middle lane. Is there any space on the shoulder in case I need to pull over? My foot feels like it's going numb, what if I can't brake if I need to?" On and on the questions kept rolling in…but I just kept on driving. I asked myself, "Is this what other people go through after having considerable procedures done? In other words, is this the way it's supposed to be? Or am I taking my life in my own hands and perhaps the life of others on the road?" Hard to say. What I know is, I have this ineffable force within me that tells me to keep going no matter what, and in time all things will balance out. So, I kept going, and eventually, it did balance out. Cruise control was great to give my leg a break. It's amazing how you can accelerate and decelerate using the cruise control instruments and drive, completely, using your hands—as long as there was no need for rapid starts and stops. I cruise-controlled the car all the way to Peterborough.

Just before I pulled into the city, I did a no-no and called Dr. Doug's office on my cell phone to see if he could take me in upon my arrival in the city. I also let his receptionist know he and I were good friends, and he told me to call. "Come on over and we'll fit you in," she replied. All I could think about on the long drive was that Dr. Doug held the key to this last piece of healing. My mind ran back to Panama and how, all along, I'd felt my problems originated from that body surfing accident. That accident, in turn, made me feel something was terribly wrong with my neck and back. That injury was the true precursor to everything that had happened since then. The doctors had tried to sort it out using drugs and invasive procedures, but inside my body I still felt the essential problem remained. Yes, my heart was beating much better and my blood pressure was improved due to allopathic intervention, but I still had those nauseous, dizzy, delirious, sickening feelings that came on from time to time. Nothing I had done in the hospital had gotten rid of that. "Thoracic angina," sounded right to me, intuitively. Just the way Dr. Doug explained it made me feel that it was the root cause of everything going down. If I could reverse the effects of that, I could turn this all around and regain my health. I was anxious to get going.

18

DÉJÀ VU

We must be willing to get rid of the life we've planned, so as to have the life that is waiting for us.

~ Joseph Campbell

"The guy who checked my lump was a Panamanian specialist, and although some of what he was saying was lost in translation, I saw the nervous look on his face. He told me to go home and get it looked at immediately." Denise relayed her disturbing recent history on our Skype call. She booked the next available flight back to Canada.

"Fuck! Not again?" I thought to myself. "Maybe this Panamanian specialist was wrong. Maybe she'll come home, get it checked, and find out the lump was benign. Maybe..." I hoped for the best, yet a part of me knew the diagnosis was correct. "Fucking cancer!" I'd been through a ton of my own trials, recently, and was totally not ready to deal with anything else—especially not what happened before. Nevertheless, times had changed, and this was a different relationship. In Lorie's case, her resentment towards me translated into a resentment toward holistic health. She showed no interest in trying any alternative methods for her cancer; she went all-in on the chemo and radiation as a means of dealing with it. It was her choice, and I did not interfere. Denise, on the other hand, was open to holistic treatments. In the past, she'd always said she would never do chemo if faced with the *C-word*. Time would tell.

When Denise returned home, things moved quickly. Before we knew it, the lump was biopsied, and it was indeed cancer; what they called *triple negative*—another aggressive strain. The doctor was advocating for a simple lump removal, and since it was on the peripheral side of her left breast, possibly removing some lymph nodes in her armpit as well. Denise, on the other hand, wanted to take the *Angelina Jolie approach* and get both breasts removed—a double mastectomy. "I don't want to get on the treadmill of having the lump removed, then the breast removed, then the other breast removed...Let's just deal with this once and for all!" she argued. I found no fault in her reasoning, having seen the prior, first-hand. In addition, she'd have to endure six, unpleasant, rounds of *dose-dense* chemotherapy. They also wanted to add in a side of radiation, but she declined. She never saw the benefit of it.

Denise hemmed and hawed about the chemotherapy. She rationalized that chemotherapy was a derivative of mustard gas, used in war. "How can that be good for your body? Not only that, chemotherapy is a proven carcinogen. Why would anyone use a cancer-causing agent to fight their cancer?" Good questions for sure. The problem was, she was getting a lot of pressure from her oncologists at the local hospital, Peterborough Regional Health Center (PRHC), to acquiesce. Her sister, Brenda Warner, a nurse at PRHC, also advocated, "Chemo's changed a lot; it isn't the severe treatment it used to be. Same for radiation, they no longer have as many mishaps and errant burning of tissue anymore."

"Hmmm...Errant burning...Good to know," I mused. Of course, I could understand Brenda's position. She wanted her sister to live, and she believed in the techniques medicine pontificated as truth—whether it made logical sense or not.

As a holistic therapist, I had worked with cancer patients before, but they were the ones sent home and told there was nothing more the system could do for them. There were also alternative cancer treatments out there, but you had to get past the browbeating of the doctors and the naysayers before you could try any of them. The pressure was simply too strong to comply. I watched as Denise was overcome, unsure of what to do. Seeing her troubling predicament, I offered a solution. We'd use holistic therapies to help recover from the devastating side effects of chemotherapy, in between treatments. At least then her own immune system would have a better chance of recovering, once the chemo sessions had concluded. That was paramount because chemo drugs destroyed your immune system. Once the treatments were over, you had nothing left to keep any small, malignant pockets from re-growing or metastasizing. She was happy with our plan, agreed to the chemo, and believed she had a fighting chance against this dreadful predator.

I set aside everything I was working on. I needed to be available to help her manage the inevitable sickness from the treatments. I also had to ensure she took the schedule of vitamins, minerals, and herbs I put together—to prophylactically protect her body from the onslaught. It was now April of 2014, and since I'd returned from Panama at the end of 2012, I had also been moonlighting with Jason's company, CONXCORP. We'd been struggling to find funding for ILLY, so both Richard and I took positions with CONXCORP to raise money. CONXCORP opened an arm of business to raise funding for humanitarian and infrastructure projects internationally. That opportunity slowed down, too. The transactions were private, so I can only say that one of the main fund providers defaulted on his ability to raise key project funds. This put the projects we'd worked on in jeopardy, and they remained in limbo while CONXCORP turned to litigation to resolve the impasse. This setback, sadly, negated our ability to generate funds for ILLY. However, the timing allowed me to switch gears and focus on the problems at home.

The holistic regimen was working well. Even Denise's oncologist commented, "You look so well. You are the poster child for chemotherapy. Keep up the good work!" The oncologist had no idea what we were doing, and we dared not tell. It seemed that anything a doctor didn't understand was forbidden. No, they wouldn't have taken any time to try to understand it; but just to be safe, don't use anything they don't know about. That was their credo, "*Do as I say, and you will be fine.*" Nevertheless, she was. Denise did the chemo, lost her hair, wore a long wig for a while, and now her hair was returning in a short, curly crop that she came to like. She was ready to move on.

After all that, I was shocked to hear she was planning on returning to Panama. She and a new friend, Kelly Fox, had started their own real estate company called *Own Panama Real Estate*. She and Kelly were partners. Denise was concerned that she had been away from the business for so long and Kelly was getting overwhelmed, doing all the work on her own. I told her, "I don't think that's wise. Although the holistic therapy treatments kept you healthy during the chemo, you need to continue with the regimen until your immune system has fully recovered."

"I will, I will!" she promised. "I'll pack up everything I need and take the herbs and stuff while I'm there. We are getting so close with a lot of the big developers. I just know a big payday is around the corner. All this is for us!" she pleaded. How could I disagree? She seemed to love the work. I recalled seeing pictures of their lawn signs, *The FoxDen Team,* shown in images of properties they represented. From where I stood, it looked like they had the potential to do very well. As long as it helped us as a family, it was a good thing. She returned to Panama in January 2015.

"Make sure your name is on a contract, and that you really are a 50-50 partner in Own Panama Real Estate," I told her. "You don't want this to end the same as Out-Of-The-Box Reading." Denise agreed, but it wasn't long before I got the news that Kelly felt Denise wasn't ready to become a 50% partner. I learned that Kelly's husband had put some money in the company and Kelly felt it should be more of a three-way split with respect to profits. Denise tried to tell me it was okay, but I knew the news had crushed her. Upon returning to Panama, she closed two or three deals right away, but that wasn't enough. She did everything she could to regain her standing in the business, to no avail. The FoxDen team was a lie, and she couldn't live with it.

Shortly after that, Denise complained of a pain in her low back. She went to a specialist in Panama, who'd suggested it was sciatica and had given her some painkillers and analgesics for the pain and inflammation. Then, one day, I got a text that Denise couldn't get out of bed! When she put pressure on her legs, they couldn't take the weight. "How did it get to that?" I questioned myself. She became bedridden, and Kelly had returned to the US for a visit home, so Denise was on her own. Thankfully, Kelly was not her only friend in Panama; Linda Tabakman and Judy Campagna were quickly on the scene. Linda helped Denise get her pain under control, packed up her things and was willing to keep, or store, the rest. Judy made plans to accompany Denise and bring her home to Canada. When she arrived at Pearson International Airport in Toronto, the night of May 17, she was in a wheelchair and couldn't walk. Thank goodness my hard work at the gym had paid off since returning home and gave me the strength to lift her into the car to drive her home to Peterborough.

Once Denise got home, I was able to see the extent of the problem. Atrophy was already setting into her legs. I immediately knew home was not the place for her. The next morning, we went straight to the ER at PRHC. The hospital ran chest X-rays, full body CT Scans, full body and brain MRIs, and still, it seemed, they were mystified with her condition.

Her sister, Brenda, was invaluable, and helped us get a room right away. She was also there, in the room, when the doctor came with the final prognosis. I watched as Brenda stood stiff and still, as if she knew something was coming, and had her fingers crossed behind her back. We were all tense as we heard the doctor say, "The cancer has returned. It's moved into your lungs, core lymph nodes, and your spinal cord in the form of *Leptomeningeal Carcinomatosis*. To simplify, the cancer has crept into your *meninges*, the jacket that protects your brain and spinal cord, and into your *cerebrospinal fluid* (CSF), the liquid inside the meninges." Everyone was stunned silent as he further went on to say, "Once in the CSF, the cancer has the potential to spur growths, as it has in the lower spine causing the sciatica-like symptoms; but it could climb up the vertebrae and into your brain, doing the same thing along the way—causing peripheral pain in other parts of your body. The only treatment, at this point, is radiation on your lower spine, to *possibly* get the use of your legs back. But even if you do get your legs back, it won't last long. The results will only be temporary." She was given four to seven months to live. A death sentence!

Denise wouldn't have it. She wasn't about to give up. The doctors felt her chances of getting any movement in her legs was bleak, even after the expected five rounds of radiation. Then a miracle took hold: first, she was able to twinkle her toes, then put a little pressure on her legs—enough to stand—then, she could make the length of the palliative care corridor with a walker. She was able to get out of bed, with assistance, and move her walker up and down the corridors successfully enough that she was discharged from palliative care. She felt she was beating the beast and was ecstatic!

"Home? I can go home!" Denise responded joyfully as the doctor discharged her, against the odds. I wasn't sure how I was going to handle it. All I knew was, I had to! During all of this, my mind often wandered back to my first wife, Lorie—how we had become so disconnected in the final months of her life. After the fact, it felt like that estrangement had damaged my relationship with her family, detrimentally. My son Nathan was still part of that family, so it was disconcerting to have things left in that way; not only for him, but for me, and possibly them, too, although it was never voiced. I was going to make sure that did not happen again.

The house became a thoroughfare as we emptied the front room on our main floor to receive shipments of a hospital bed, two walkers, a wheelchair, two commodes, and medical supplies. Then, the revolving door began with Personal Support Workers, the Occupational Therapist, the Physical Therapist, Hospice volunteers, her Nurse, and her Doctor. Denise was flourishing.

She was even able to make it up and down the stairs, with assistance...Until one day she couldn't! I remember that day well, because it was the turning point. The stairs represented her level of strength, and her strength was tied to her willpower. The moment the strength began to wane, so too did the willpower. Along with the waning of the willpower, came the need for more, and stronger, pain medications. We couldn't reach the doctors quick enough for the repeated increases in hydromorphone doses. We even tried medical marijuana, but the combination of medical MJ with high doses of hydromorphone only seemed to whack her out, such that her speech was unintelligible. She needed to be readmitted to palliative care, and on July 30th it was so. Having left the hospital on July 6, she was able to enjoy almost a month at home.

From then on, we both lived at the hospital. Okay, she lived there, in palliative care, but I was there from the time I awoke until the time she went to sleep. The only time I wasn't there was to go home, meditate to rebalance myself, then sleep to regenerate enough to do it all over again. I knew all the doctors and nurses on a first name basis. Whilst friends and family came and went, sad and teary-eyed, I kept my composure. I'd learned that those approaching death don't want to see the pain and suffering they will leave behind; they needed to know everything would be okay. That is what freed them to leave, when the time came. I don't know how many times I was asked, "How are you able to deal with this every day? Why is this not breaking you down?" The simple answer was, "Because I can't! The time will come for breaking down, but that time isn't now. I need to be strong for her." I needed to be strong this time, because I wasn't able to, before. I'd been given a second chance to do things right, and I wasn't going to fuck it up again. Time to put up or shut up!

Denise's goal was to make it to her father's, Hayward MacDonald's, birthday on August 13th. The next goal was her daughter's, Ariana's, birthday on the 17th. She made both of those. She also wanted to be lucid when the final moments came, but once the metastases moved into her brain, she was often found talking to, and seeing things, in another realm while, simultaneously, talking to those in the room. They couldn't understand what was going on, but to me, it was normal. Some chuckled uneasily, but somehow I comprehended it all and spoke to her understandingly, as if it were normal. Then, the strong headaches began to hit, and we were forced to sedate her more fully. Overnight, her breathing began to slow, and to gurgle. Family began taking turns staying overnight. On the final night, her sisters, Brenda and Janet Mahood, her daughters, Ariana and Melissa, and her *bff*, Karen Lunn, camped out in the hospital for the vigil, and I went home to recover, as usual.

In the morning, I awoke and got up earlier than usual, around 6 a.m.. Something was telling me to get ready. As I hopped out of the shower, I got a call to come to the hospital right away because Denise's breathing had taken a turn. When I got there, everyone was in the room—somber and quiet. After I exchanged hugs and whispered pleasantries, I took my place beside the head of the bed. I noticed the new, raspy, gurgling sound emanating from her lungs, and the long period between her breaths—almost a minute. She was hanging on by a thin thread. I leaned in toward her and whispered. "I'm here now. Everything is okay. You don't have to hold on anymore. We all love you. Time to let go." Then her eyes, which had been half-open for quite some time, opened fully as she looked up to the third eye center and released her last breath of air, slowly hissing like a tire tube going flat, and she was gone. Then it came. The sadness, anxiety, anger, resentment, and grief that I'd been holding onto for so long came out, all at once, in a gut-wrenching deluge of tears. What everyone watched for, and seemed to be waiting for from me, manifested into a sobbing mess that went around and hugged each of them individually. Everyone was in tears. Her parents, Hayward and Margaret, appeared on the scene shortly after that, to join in. They had also been called but, sadly, didn't make it there in time. She'd waited for me, then entered the pearly gates on August 24, 2015, shortly after my arrival.

Once again, the packing up. It always amazed me, once someone had passed away, the immediacy in which the family must vacate the room. Yes, I knew, they needed the room—but still! Everyone chipped in and bagged up all of Denise's possessions, then I placed it all in my car. Her parents invited me to their home where everyone would be gathering, but I graciously declined saying, "I've got a few errands to run." As somewhat of an introvert, a private person, my role as host to the seemingly never-ending multitude of family and guests had ended. I needed to get grounded. I drove straight to the gym, and, thanks to my years of training and memorized workout routines, robotically went through the paces—as if I were in a dream, a trance. My job wasn't completely over. With Lorie's death, her family took care of everything, but this one was on me. With the assistance of Ariana, along with the help of a family friend Teresa Consentino, a chaplain with one of the local high schools, we'd previously picked out the venue, cremation urn, family keepsakes, and procedures for the event to come. All that was left was to contact the funeral home director to get the ball rolling. It was so.

Denise got the spotlight one last time. I knew she wouldn't have wanted a *run-of-the-mill* funeral, but a *Celebration of Life!* She got that. More than 500 people filled the parking lot and nearby streets to pay their respects. Friends from near and far, Canada and Panama, sent in snippets of video that my sister and her husband, Paula and Tony, lovingly remastered into a Celebration of Life video tribute. Video played in one sitting room, while others watched a commemorative photo stream, ate snacks and drank coffee, tea, or libations, in a larger receiving room. Additionally, guests paid their respects to her in an open-casket viewing room, prior to her final cremation. The event was a great success! Denise looked down and smiled, from heaven.

PART IV

IN TUNE WITH DIVINE WILL

2015 - 2019

19

THIRD TIME'S THE CHARM

*The more we live guided from within, the greater our control over
outer events in the great game of life.*

~ Paramahansa Yogananda

After Denise's death, I needed to begin expanding my life
again. While she was in palliative care at PRHC, my life
contracted—significantly! I simplified and reduced almost
everything in my life—business, home, friends. It was all shut
down to be there for her. Now, I needed to rekindle my life and
get going again!

When I got back into the house at the end of 2012, I was
home alone, meditating, rehabilitating at the gym, taking care
of myself. In the summer of 2013, Nathan came home from
Panama for a visit. He'd made many friends at the Panama Coast
International School (PCIS) and had fully expected to return.
During the summer, he got reacquainted with his old friends
from Peterborough and was torn between returning and staying.
He played in the summer *Hoop Dreams* basketball camp and was
reminded of how much he loved the game. That, and missing his
father of course, cemented his decision to remain in Canada. That
fall, given that PCIS had an English curriculum, he transferred

seamlessly to St. Peter's Secondary School in Peterborough. Prior to moving to Panama, I had always assistant-coached Nathan's basketball teams, so it was time to throw that hat back on. Now, the 2015/2016 season was getting underway. Twice-weekly practices, tournaments every weekend, things got busy—fast! I reconnected with the Peterborough Power coach, and good friend, Joe Hadzi, and re-established my position as assistant coach. Time to get going once again.

I also met up with my friend Doug Lukinuk, or *Dr. Doug* as he was commonly known. He had invented a device to help patients with *text (or tech) neck syndrome*: a forward head posture from too much time sitting in front of computers or staring down at mobile devices. I was excited for him to get going on this project, knowing how much chiropractic had helped me when I returned home in 2012. After everything that had happened to me in the hospital in 2012, I still had pain in my neck, back, and chest. When those areas were locked up, they produced fearful, sickly feelings, meanwhile draining my body of all energy. The hospital and its doctors had done everything they could, but it was still there. Dr. Doug called it thoracic angina, often called *cervicothoracic angina,* characterized by decreased or aberrant motion of involved spine segments—C4 to C7 or T1 to T8. It was also commonly caused by *trauma,* or excessive strain, on the involved joints. "Yep, I definitely suffered a trauma to my neck and upper back," I thought. "Sounds like we're on the right track." Once I had my first chiropractic manipulation, like a gift from heaven, all the fear, pain, and suffering melted away. I floated peacefully...for a moment. The effects were not lasting. Doug explained that his treatment gave me a taste of the good health I could regain once my nervous system returned to normal. The damage had been locked-in, having been left untreated all that time. I needed regular, sustained treatments, declining over time, to fix the problem. "I'm in. Where do I sign up?" I started off with three treatments a week for six weeks, two per week for four weeks, then once a week until my treatment package was exhausted. It worked! I still had some soft tissue issues from time to time, but overall, my nervous system was working much better.

This time, however, I was here to help him—to return the favor. He had a busy chiropractic practice and no time to work on his device. He asked me if I could help, pick the project up off the floor, get a prototype built, and get things going. With the rise of technology, and the problems he was seeing in his practice, he knew the product would be a huge success. "Why not?" I thought. "My good friend and ILLY business partner, Richard, is an engineer. We could do this!" I'd brought Rich into ILLY, which had now slowed down to a snail's crawl. Bringing him into this project was my way of paying him back. Being back in a mode of expansion, I now had a new business project to focus my energies on.

I also used this expansion time to go deeper in meditation. My guru, Paramahansa Yogananda, said something to the effect of, "If the devotee (devoted student) practices Kriya yoga, morning and night, for eight years consecutively, his life will change in ways he cannot imagine." That's what I wanted, and needed, and had set out to do when I picked up my meditation practice back in Panama. That was 2011, and now it was 2016; five years down, three more to go. I was now practising 72 Kriyas morning and night, including two mudras (a symbolic pose) that involved 12 more Kriyas, for a total of 84 Kriyas. I loved the idea that each Kriya breath was equivalent to one year of spiritual living. Therefore 84 Kriyas was like 84 years of spiritual living, or the equivalent of one lifetime, twice daily. It's like I was evolving more spiritually at the rate of two lifetimes per day. I could feel it, too! The reason I chose Kriya yoga was that, originally being of scientific mind, I needed to prove to myself that the method worked. I wasn't asked to blindly believe that Kriya yoga was truly the *jet plane method* to self-realization, I was told to try it for myself, then judge. I did.

Yogananda once asked of a habit-riddled man who was interested in the practice, "Do you smoke cigarettes?"

The man answered, "Yes."

Yogananda replied, "You can do that." Yogananda then asked him, "Do you drink alcohol?"

The man replied, "Yes."

Yogananda said, "You can do that." Then, Yogananda asked the man, "Do you have relations with the opposite sex?"

The man responded, "Yes."

Yogananda said again, "You can do that…" He then went on to say "But, you may find that you do not want to do these things so much anymore."

That is the beauty of Kriya yoga. I personally found that many of my own habits had gone by the wayside over time. Would those habits have disappeared otherwise? I think not. I've looked around and seen many people that I'd known from the past—high school friends, neighborhood buddies, workmates, you name it—still drinking, smoking, and partying like they had when I knew them many years ago. I'd probably still be doing the same things, too, but most likely, I'd be dead. If I hadn't woken up to change, I might now be in heaven…but most likely hell. I attributed my good fortune to the changes I'd made spiritually, and wouldn't be here today without them.

"What good fortune?" You may ask. "A heart and kidney transplant, you lost two wives, and you almost lost your own life multiple times. What good fortune?"

My response to that is "I am where I am in this life, not in spite of the things that have happened, but *because of them!*" I now, regularly, experienced true happiness and joy and recognized that these emotions came from within; I struggled to find them before because I looked for them outside of myself. That is my good fortune! Priceless!

In time, I met a wonderful soul named Salome Shyan on a dating site named Zoosk. Once again, I respectfully waited for an appropriate amount of time to pass before I even looked toward the opposite sex. After I created my online profile, I was matched with women who exuded the characteristics I was looking for. In the past, my focus was on physical attributes. Now, those attributes, while still important, took a backseat to candidates who were more spiritually minded. If you've never been on one of these sites, you're able to see profile pictures of the individuals you're matched with. That way, you dispensed with the ones who didn't tickle your fancy and focused on the ones who did. Some members either didn't want to, or couldn't be bothered to, upload a profile picture. Those matches always went to the trash. "If you're on a dating site, how do you expect to attract someone if you don't even upload a picture of yourself?" I thought. Each member was also identified by a username, which protected one's anonymity and privacy.

One day, one of those blank profiles said, "Hi." Her username was *dancing gratitude*. I was just about to send this blank match into oblivion, but instead I had an intuitive sense about the username.

"Hmmm… dancing gratitude, eh?" Against my better judgement, I replied "Hi, how are you? It would be great if you could upload a picture of yourself," and left it at that. I waited a couple of days, and no reply. "Okay, whatever!" Then, it was there—a photo: a snowy, outside, winter shot; she was wearing a long, black, down-filled coat and had a strange smile on her face, as if someone was taking her picture and she didn't want to. It probably wasn't the first-choice photo for a dating profile. Still, something intrigued me. Intuitively, I saw through the photo into someone who was shy, and while on a dating site to attract a mate, really didn't want to be there. I could understand that. I, too, was questioning whether I wanted another relationship. Abstention was a much more sure-fire way of deepening one's relationship with God. My path would have been easier on my own, but something about the shyness and the gratitude piece intrigued me, so I pressed on. We chatted online, had a couple of phone calls, then decided to meet in person.

I'll never forget the bright ear-to-ear smile, draped in a long, dark brown, almost-black-haired countenance that greeted me when I entered the Chapters bookstore in Peterborough. I had just entered the front doors, looked to the right, and she was coming forward to greet me. Her radiant smile captivated me, and even then, I knew there was something special about this woman. We found two seats at a small table, ordered two teas, and got to know each other. She had two kids: Misha, 15, and Phoebe, 12. She spoke of: her draw to India, having been there a number of times in her youth, her vocation, a geriatric mental health nurse, and that she loved yoga and meditation—a woman after my own heart. We met again over the next few days. It felt like God had a hand in choosing the right match for me. Yes, the path to God is easier on one's own, but it can also be done as a *householder*, and it felt as though I had been given the blessing to do so.

Everything was expanding in my life, and eventually that expansion hit Illy, too. During my contracted period, Richard was busy in the background, reaching out to web development and marketing firms to find an individual or company who could ramp us up. During that down period, Lyriq had moved on from the board of directors, to more fully pursue his acting career that had taken off. That left a vacuum—a space to be filled. In stepped Gurminder Kandola and CTO Boost. At the time, Gurminder was also the Chief Technology Officer (CTO) and Head of Product at *Diply* and was thought to have been instrumental in their phenomenal success. Diply was ranked among the top 100 most popular websites in the world and the top 20 websites in Canada. Kings of clickbait content, the company was averaging 41 million unique visitors each month. "Forty-one million unique visitors each month!" I thought. "Imagine if we had just a small percentage of that, Illy would blow up!" Not only did Gurminder want to partner with Illy, he also introduced Illy to the top dogs at Diply—and they were interested. It seemed like a match made in heaven, and I couldn't wait for it to get its wings.

Life was getting busy again. Business opportunities, great relationship, fitness improving, getting out of the house to coach basketball, travelling around Ontario for games and tournaments—life was good. My rapport with the transplant team was the best it had been in years. I was down to one biopsy every six months, and after the one scheduled for next week, I was hoping to go to one biopsy per year. They were even letting me do my quarterly echocardiograms at the local cardiology clinic in Peterborough. I'd just come from one and was waiting for the follow-up call from my transplant team in Toronto. The only real threat I had to watch for, regularly, was the average cold or flu. Being immune suppressed, it was harder for me to fight off even the simple bugs that plagued everyone else temporarily. I seemed to have picked up a flu bug around that time and was hitting it with everything I knew—nascent iodine, colloidal silver, oregano oil, and increasing my pH with bicarbonates. Still, I had a temperature and the odd chills, tightness in the chest, felt heavy, lethargic, and struggled to stand or walk for moderate periods of time. It was a doozy.

"Hi Kirk, it's Stella. I'm calling about your recent echocardiogram. How are you doing?" I went on to tell her that I had the flu, and it was kicking me to the curb. "That's not the flu!" She replied. "Your echo results show changes in your heart, maybe even possible rejection. How soon can you get to the hospital?"

"Rejection? What the…fffff'k Again? What now?" I thought quietly to myself, then offered, "I've got a biopsy next week, November 9, 2016. Will that work?" At the time, I didn't see the urgency of it. This was all *old hat* and I had no desire to be locked away in the hospital anytime soon. We agreed upon the plan and the call ended.

Since my first heart transplant, I'd traveled to my early-morning biopsies on my own. First, Lorie was too sick to accompany me, then Denise was in Panama; there was always a reason why I traveled alone. The hospital required you to have a companion who picked you up and took you home after biopsies, but I didn't say anything, and nobody asked. To be there for 7 a.m. meant getting up at 5 a.m. to get to TGH from Peterborough. What a pain in the butt! The other alternative was to drive down the night before, have a visit with my mom in Toronto, crash at her place, then make the much easier 20-minute drive to TGH. While it was enjoyable visiting with my mom, again, I was putting her out. This time was different. Salome was coming with me and wouldn't take no for an answer. "You shouldn't be going to these important procedures alone! I'm going with you, and from now on, you won't be going alone." Music to my ears. I had my first heart transplant at the age of 35. At that age, I was strong and recovered from procedures more quickly. At 51, after all the medical interventions, that strength was beginning to wane. It took longer to heal and recover. I was grateful that Salome was with me.

TGH had relationships with local hotels, so we booked a hospital-rate room for November 8th at the Chelsea Hotel, a stone's throw from the TGH. We headed down to Toronto to check in just after dinner. Shortly after arriving, we thought we'd enjoy a hot tea at the café on the main floor. While sitting, enjoying our tea, I got a funny feeling in my chest. Salome looked over, noticed the strange look on my face and asked if I was okay. I couldn't respond right away. I was silently rapt in my chair, tuned in, listening to my heart. I hadn't been this body-conscious for a long time so, at first, I thought I just wasn't able to tune in. I went deeper and searched for any sound emanating from my chest but couldn't find one. "Something isn't right," I finally said to Salome after the long, drawn-out stare. "We are so close to the hospital, maybe we should walk over there now."

"Walk? Can you walk? Should I call an ambulance?" Salome countered.

After another moment of contemplation, "No, I'll make it," I replied. Did I actually know if I could make it? I wasn't totally sure. That fool of an ego always had something to say. "I'm a block-and-a-half from the emergency wing of the large, city-block-wide hospital. What a fool I'd look like, to have an ambulance show up, roll in the stretcher, put me on, buckle me up, sirens blazing, to drive 500 meters. Wimp!" I couldn't have that. I would've felt foolish indeed. But what would've been more foolish would've been to attempt the walk, suffer an event, then crumple up and die on the sidewalk 50 meters from the ER entrance. Huge fail! I couldn't have that either. Something inside me told me I would be okay, so we walked…Super slowly…Not caring about what anyone thought…Until we arrived at our destination…Still alive!

Over the last many years, I'd had the necessity to show up at the emergency department of hospitals both in Peterborough and Toronto, but this was the fastest I ever made it through the guardians of the gate—the intake soldiers—so quickly. I told the male receptionist I was a heart transplant recipient, that I had a scheduled biopsy the next day, and was expected to be admitted afterward because of the results of an abnormal echo I'd done about a month ago. Within moments, another nurse came to get me, and in I went. No messing around. Time to find out what this was all about.

20

T2: JUDGEMENT DAY

If you are still breathing, you have a second chance.

~ Oprah Winfrey

" ...We feel that putting a stent into the blocked coronary artery is *high-risk*. Alternatively, since after all these years you remain so robust, we feel you're a good candidate for a *second heart transplant*. Give it some thought and let me know what you think," Dr. Ross concluded.

"A second heart transplant. Already?" I'd always hoped I would be blessed enough to be one of the longest-living heart transplant survivors...but that was with the first transplanted heart, not two combined! Yes, I'd contemplated I might receive a second heart transplant at some point in the future. Just not now. Yet, here it was. The decision was right before me.

The day after being admitted, I had my heart biopsy with Dr. Daley followed by an echocardiogram and an angiogram the following day. Initially, it was felt that one of two things caused this: antibodies had attacked my left ventricle; or occlusions had built up in my coronary arteries, starving off my heart graft from the oxygen it craved via the blood supply. If it was antibodies, or low *ejection fraction*[vii] as noted from the echo, the solution would be immunological. Whereas if it was a narrowing or an occlusion, another stent could be put in to relieve the problem, or a combination of the two. Those were the first solutions I'd been presented with by Dr. Daley. His sentiments were also echoed by the many doctors I saw over the next few days—heavily leaning on the stent option. I, too, came to hope that the solution would be to pop another stent in then send me merrily on my way. Still, this *high-risk* opinion was pervasive. What were the doctors worrying about?

Apparently, the artery that needed to be stented was a large one, which fed *three* clusters of coronary arteries. Normally, each cluster should have had its own large-artery supply. One supply was blocked in 2010, which I knew about, but now a third cluster was relying on that same artery. The high-risk element of the stent procedure was if this single, large artery—which was feeding the three clusters—collapsed, my heart could go into shock, damage my kidneys, and bringing the whole house of cards tumbling down. Aside from the obvious *death* that could occur, the disaster could also disqualify me from any opportunity of a second heart transplant. That's when it was first debated that a second heart transplant was the safer option. "Safe is good!" I thought I'd better grab it up…While I still could!

After that, everything moved quickly. I was bounced from one transplant-workup test to another: breathing capacity, muscle strength, even cognitive tests. The transplant team had to make sure I was a suitable candidate for T2 (my nickname for heart transplant #2). I was back in the CICU, where the cardiac team was busily working to reduce my fluid levels. Within a couple of weeks, I had dropped 20 pounds. Notwithstanding that weight loss, my next right-heart-catheter biopsy showed that the pressures had gone up! "How can that be? I feel like I'm bone dry. Can there really be more fluid hiding somewhere in my body, putting pressure on my heart?" What I was really worried about, was whether the pressures would come down at all. If the pressures were not correct, between the heart and the lungs, it would destroy any new heart graft. They just wouldn't allow that. They wouldn't move ahead without acceptable pressures. Time was running out!

During all of this, I was also placed on a number of IV-drip medications that kept my heart beating more forcefully while I waited for the transplant. The first drug we tried caused my heart to go into tachycardia, beating at 160 bpm, in the middle of the night. It was like one of those medical TV shows, where you hear the conspicuous *code blue* call over the PA system, and the team comes busting into the room with the crash cart. It was just like that, except without the fanfare. The nurses came in and explained to me that my heart was in *supraventricular tachycardia,* and they needed to bring my heart rate down. They had to wait for the doctor to come to inject *adenosine* into my IV line. They then went on to tell me to "Be prepared, once the adenosine hits. According to what other patients have said, you will feel like you're dying, floating away. The adenosine should bring your heart rate back to normal, but it could also stop your heart. In which case, we'll have the paddles here ready to bring you back!"

"Death? Paddles? Unbelievable..." I'd watched way too much TV in my lifetime; I had a graphic idea of what this might end like. Still, a peace came over me. Death was something I practiced every day in meditation; or more precisely, the *deathless state*. I decided I would calmly relax and slip into that space. If death came, I'd be none the wiser. It would simply be a peaceful experience.

The resident doctor showed up and injected the adenosine. Sure enough, everything slowed...down...to a...nothingness. "Mr. Johnson? Are you there? Mr. Johnson?" my nurse called out!

I opened my eyes, and replied calmly, "Yes, I'm here."

"You didn't move. We weren't sure if you were still with us. Your heart rate has returned to normal. Everything is okay," the nurse clarified.

"I'm good" I replied. "In preparing for the possibility of going out, I went into a meditative state to reduce the impact. It all felt okay."

In the morning when Salome returned, I told her what had happened. Visitors were not allowed to stay with patients in the CICU overnight. Salome had found a bed-and-breakfast nearby that she stayed at, periodically, until she found a place through a friend of her mother. Other than that, she was with me every moment of every day—the quintessential caregiver, while in a dark place. She felt horrible that she wasn't with me in my time of need. The following night, the same thing happened. This time my nurse asked, "Please, while I know going into your meditative state is good for you, it really freaks us out. So please, try to keep your eyes open this time around." The adenosine worked again, thankfully, and that was the end of drug number one. On to the next drug, dobutamine, the same drug that had sustained me for six months prior to T1. It worked, for a while…

Among other things, the doctors also added nitroglycerin into the fold, as a vasodilator, to open the blood pathways. I imagine it did its job, but it also opened some serious, brain-splitting, migraine-like headaches. I complained of it every moment I had the chance and was given painkillers, but they barely touched it. They begged me to stay on it. It was a necessary evil for success. It paid off! My next biopsy came around and, by the grace of God, the pressures had come down; the second-to-last hurdle to getting listed for T2. I breathed a sigh of relief. The last hurdle was still part of the transplant workup: a visit from the transplant team psychologist. I had heard through the grapevine that she was a tough cookie, the last line of defence before the goal line. I was ready for her.

The job of the transplant team psychologist was to put the scare of God into you. She was to make sure you followed all the rules: keep your fluid levels low while waiting, report any sickness you may have while waiting, follow all the doctors' instructions, and lastly, take *all of your medications* and on time. The last one was the one she was trying to drive home with me. She had my chart and history and we reviewed what happened back in late 2012. I knew she held the keys to the kingdom, and I had to humble myself, explain my position appropriately, and agree to everything she asked for. Like a young schoolboy in the principal's office, I took my slaps on the wrist and showed my best face of atonement, hurriedly, because I couldn't wait to get to recess, outside, and play with my friends. Once her role as scaremonger was satisfied, her tone changed completely and she asked, "By the way, how *did* you manage to keep your first heart for 16 years? Very impressive, considering the average at that time was nine years. Quite an accomplishment!"

"Thank you," I replied. I could have said more, but I chose to consider her question rhetorical. To answer it truthfully would've gone against many of the terms I agreed to earlier. She really didn't want to know all the holistic and spiritual practices that kept me alive for so long. Even with the stopping of the meds back in Panama, my healthful practices kept me *waaaay* ahead of the game. In retrospect, I wouldn't do it again. I now understood my mistake regarding death and the deathless state. My promise to the psychologist wasn't lip service. I promised to toe the line, and I meant it!

While on the dobutamine, I needed to stay in the CICU. The situation was beginning to look a whole lot like my first transplant in that I would have to live in the hospital until T2 became available. Then, one night, the dobutamine also sent me into tachycardia. In came the crash cart. In went the adenosine. On came the feeling of death. Down came my heart rate, and I was back to normal. After three rounds of tachycardia with the dobutamine, the doctors finally decided to wean me off of IV meds and, albeit slim, see if there was a possibility that I could go home to wait for T2, taking comparable oral medications instead.

It was one week before Christmas 2016. As you could imagine, all I wanted from Santa was T2, but as the season drew nearer I would've settled for being discharged—to wait for the life-saving organ outside of the hospital. Overall, I was pleased with myself; I'd endured the past few weeks with limited negative encounters of any kind. Nevertheless, once again, I had my fill of the poking, prodding, and near-death experiences; enough for a lifetime—all in one mega-dose. Thankfully, as luck would have it, I got my second wish: I was getting out! As a condition of leaving the hospital, I had to have a defibrillator implanted—painfully—and gained a new appreciation for Percocet. With my oral meds balanced, and off all IV meds, the defibrillator was implanted as a precautionary resource: a *just-in-case*. I was discharged to wait for T2 in the comfort of my own home. Ho-ho-ho! Merry Christmas to me!

Being on the transplant list for the second time, or any time, was a mercurial thing. You could be removed for something as simple as a common cold. As such, I was doing my best to avoid too much contact with the outside world. Having dropped so much weight while in the hospital, and with the need to avoid illness, I had to dispense with my go-to solution for recovery: the gym. While the cleaners did a good job cleaning the machines at GoodLife, the place was still a veritable smorgasbord of germs and microbes. "Time to set up a small gym of our own, in the house!" We splurged and picked up a decent treadmill to go along with the electronic stationary bike Salome brought over when we combined households. I was determined to be in the best shape possible for T2. I was in such good shape that after a routine echocardiogram, Stella called to tell me my ejection fraction was at 60%—normal. She then went on to ask if I was willing to look at different options, other than T2. My mind ran back to the CICU. Salome, while pacing the halls, came across a woman whose husband was in a room two doors down from mine. It seemed, a couple years earlier, her husband had come to the hospital with a situation similar to my own, needing a heart transplant. However, in his case, they patched him up, got him better, and he was able to go home, happy and content. Now, two years later, he was back in the hospital, but his heart and his health had deteriorated so much that he was no longer a candidate for a transplant. Now his family was waiting for him to die in the CICU; a medical tragedy. Needless to say, my answer to Stella was firm, "No, I've come this far. Let's finish what we started!"

Due to my high level of antibodies, I was high priority. I had moved beyond the provincial, to the national, registry. The doctors suggested the wait might only be six weeks, but it was now May 2017—five months since being released from the hospital. I was so grateful I got out of there. Gratitude was a powerful thing. If you were grateful for the little things in your life, you'd be blessed with more things to be grateful for. A cyclical process that fed upon itself. The law of attraction at its best. My gratitude paid off! On May 8, I got the call. Salome and my son, Nathan, were so nervous, neither of them wanted to drive to the hospital. I on the other hand, had recovered so well and felt so good, we grabbed our pre-packed bags and I drove us all to the hospital for my own heart transplant. "A beast!" in the millennial vernacular.

Within moments of being admitted, I was back in the CICU waving to the staff like the celebrity walking the red carpet to the Oscars, smiling at the onlookers and momentarily posing for camera shots. Next, I removed my street clothes and donned the customary light blue smock. Then, it was off to another room to get a line inserted. In the CICU, they don't have a Cath Lab, just a rudimentary, ad hoc room where the residents practiced putting lines in—almost blind, since they didn't have a monitor to check their progress. And they wanted to access the left side… into the candy-cane pass…I gave them all the warnings, as I had in the past. In the end, all I could do was chuckle affably as they poked, apologized, re-poked, and apologized to no avail. Having been told that it was my last, working, entry point for biopsies, they backed off, saying that, "A line can be put in—while you're under—in the operating room."

"Why didn't they just let that happen in the first place?" I mused. By now, I'm sure you can guess the answer to that. *Free meat!*

My family was beginning to gather, waiting to see me off. Somehow, this gathering was a lively one. No morose faces looking down on me, as had happened for T1. Perhaps, over the years, my family having seen me at my worst, and yet somehow always rising to the challenge, was filled with hope. "This is just another routine procedure for Kirk. We'll see him soon!"

In the operating room, I was greeted by Dr. Vivek Rao, Chief of Cardiovascular Surgery—the big dog. "How are you?" he asked. "Are you ready to go?"

"Yes, all good," I replied. I looked around. Lying flat on the operating table, it was difficult to get the lay of the land; there were so many masked specialists busily working away. It was never long before one of them came up and asked you to count to 10. I began, "One, two…" Out! Being under anaesthetic was different than sleep, a seizure, even death; all of these were altered states, in which the mind was still switched on. When put out fully, like under anaesthetic, there was no thought, no mind, no nothing, not even darkness. Just missed time.

Much of what happened next, was retold to me by Salome. After I came out of the surgery, it took a long time for me to come around. They were poking my toes to see if I'd wake up, but I remained in that comatose state until I was *good and ready to come out*. Sounds like me! After that, remembering my story of the troubles I'd had being intubated and not able to breathe fully after T1, Salome asked them to remove the long tube as soon as it was possible. Travis and Nathan were both there and I told them they could stay. They soon scurried out, though, not wanting to see the tube get pulled out—like Arnold Schwarzenegger's *Predator*, tearing the spine out of its victims. Gruesome or not, my only thought was, "Ahhh! To breathe once again."

Unfortunately, I was informed that my kidneys remained stunned from the surgery, and that I would need dialysis *until* they began operating again. Like the boomerang you thought you had thrown away for good, in came the dialysis machine. I'm not sure why, but it didn't bother me this time. Maybe I was too whacked out to care, or maybe I knew it would only be for a few days. Who knew? Maybe, I was beginning to become comfortable in my own skin and realized that everything that was being done was for my highest good? All I had to do, was let it be. As I came in and out of consciousness, I could see two young ladies busily working around the dialysis machine. One moment there was one nurse, then two, then two nurses along with a supervisor; something had gone wrong! It seemed a considerable amount of my blood was trapped and coagulated inside the dialyzer. The supervisor was chastising the two younger nurses. As the dialysis crew bickered away, my recovery room nurse informed us that I would need a blood transfusion, along with a bag of IV iron, to correct the problem. My hemoglobin and energy stores were bottoming out!

"How could this happen?" I wondered. Salome then reminded me that prior to the surgery, a clinician had come around with a form that I ended up signing. Seemed that after T1, I had troubles with thin blood. Now they had a solution to that; a new product that would cause the blood to thicken more readily after the surgery. Made sense at the time, but now I was questioning, "Hmmm...I signed up for a new, high-tech product designed to thicken my blood more quickly, and now my blood has jammed up the dialysis machine?" It made total sense to me why this was happening, but no one was even considering it. "Mums the word, and par for the course," I thought. Then I remembered I was in *go-with-the-flow mode* and just let it pass.

There had always been a threat that my transplanted kidney would not survive the corporeal gymnastics of the heart transplant operation. Prior to the operation, Dr. Ross had painstakingly communed with the renal transplant department heads to ensure there was a plan in place in case that happened. Thankfully, by the grace of God, within a few days the kidney bounced back—like a champ! I wasn't sad to see the dialysis machine go. By then, all my tubes had been removed, including a wire that remained connected to my heart after the defibrillator was removed during the transplant surgery. It stung like heck coming out! I was weaned off all the IV drugs; they were replaced by oral drugs I would continue to take at home. While at times I struggled, having been the proverbial *pincushion* for 20 years, I had to say, medicine had evolved to be a truly spectacular thing. Yes, there were a few errors here and there, but after only 12 days of hospital stay, having received a second life-saving heart transplant, I was able to go home. Kudos to the team at the Toronto General Hospital. *Full props!*

21

THE LIGHT COMES ON!

Keep your thoughts positive because your thoughts become your words. Keep your words positive because your words become your behavior. Keep your behavior positive because your behavior becomes your habits. Keep your habits positive because your habits become your values. Keep your values positive because your values become your destiny.

~ Mahatma Gandhi

"It's going to be really tough!" The words echoed repeatedly, like a shout reverberating in the *Grand Canyon*. Dr. Carolina Alba had made that statement when I decided to go for T2. At that time, I never thought to ask her what she meant, but now I was beginning to understand. I was now 52, and healing occurred more slowly in my body than when I was 35. After the dialysis blood-coagulation incident, my hemoglobin remained low; I felt weak and lethargic all the time. That meant very little rehab: no treadmill, no stationary bike. My go-to system for recovery was severely hampered.

I set up a small bookshelf beside my living room La-Z-Boy chair. It had everything I needed: two drug organizers, syringes, a sharps container, vials of saline, assorted bandages—you name it—and most importantly, the TV controller! The bookshelf also contained my charts, which were reviewed weekly by my home nurse. The nurse was needed to oversee my operation of an inhaler twice daily to inhale a yellow drug called amphotericin B: an antifungal to prevent lung infections after heart transplant. I needed the syringes to inject enoxaparin subcutaneously, in the area below my belly button, to get rid of two clots that formed after removing my PICC line (peripherally inserted central catheter) prior to hospital release. The two clots were tolerable during the day but tormented me at night. They woke me up constantly with deep, throbbing pain. Lastly, I needed gauze and tape to soak up the two leaks that had sprung from my groin area. After all the punctures in my groin for biopsies, angiograms, etc., one day, the scabs popped open and a clear fluid began running down my legs, constantly. This went on for weeks. I even tried men's incontinence diapers to absorb the deluge but soaked through a few of those daily. Finally, I had to reinforce them with absorbent gauze pads. I totally felt like I was in the movie "You Don't Mess with the Zohan!" with *the big bush*! *Super embarrassing*!

Unlike after T1, I decided not to stay in Toronto for my follow-up biopsies. With Salome by my side, she took time off work and we made the trips like *Road Warriors*. On June 2, 2017, I'd had two weekly biopsies and both procedures turned up negative for rejection. I would need to have a couple more weekly biopsies, then they would drop to biweekly, then monthly etc. Each biopsy provided an opportunity to titrate down the heavy doses of anti-rejection meds and steroids to more normal levels. I had already reduced my prednisone twice and was very happy about that. I hated the stuff!

Once again meditating regularly, God always sent me what I needed; the benefit of being connected. The last match was perfect. T1 left me with a ton of antibodies to counter against matching further suitable organs: 96 out of 100 to be exact. The doctors informed me that there were no negative implications to the heart that I received. In other words, the heart was not compromised by even 1 of the 96 antibodies that might stir rejection. What were the odds? It felt like winning the lottery!

My transplant team was reluctant to reduce the immunosupressive drugs too quickly. "If we move too fast, and your biopsy shows rejection, we will be forced to start the whole process all over again. That will make things take much longer," was the refrain I heard repeatedly. The result of that slow withdrawal was the bottoming out of my white blood cell count. Being both immune suppressed, as well as having a low white count made me more susceptible to everyday pathogens. It took over a year for the white count to come close to resembling normal. During that time, I stayed inside. I rarely left the house, except for medical appointments. I became a shut-in. The transplant team disagreed with this methodology, but I wasn't taking any chances. Being an introvert, that didn't bother me too much. In fact, it worked out well because it gave my body time to rest—especially my hip and right leg.

Somewhere along the transplant workup and surgery pathway, I began having deep aches and pains in my body: predominantly my neck, shoulders, hips, and legs. The pain was so nagging, I couldn't fall asleep, and when I did, it wasn't a restful sleep. The lack of sleep exacerbated the problem into a nightmare. I complained to the transplant team at TGH, who then passed me on to my GP, who then passed me on to the pain clinic back at TGH; what you'd call *the runaround*. Even the pain clinic couldn't determine the cause of the problem. Yes, they understood that after a second heart transplant, along with the side effects of a declining kidney graft, many abnormalities were possible. In the end, they gave me pain killers and muscle relaxants to help soothe, but not solve, the problems. Time, with a little rehab, was the remedy. In time, some of the problems dissipated. The neck and the shoulder issues subsided, leaving only pain starting at my right hip and running down the peripheral side of my leg into my foot. These last, lingering issues wouldn't go away; they continued to ache throughout the night.

In October 2019, two and a half years post T2, I had exhausted the efficacy of my home gym and decided it was time to return to GoodLife. "Maybe I need to push my body a little harder," I wondered. "That might be just what I need: to strengthen my legs and hips to get rid of this pain. It's what I've always done in the past: push through. Why shouldn't it work now?" Back I went. I was cognizant enough to go slow and ramp up, nice and easy. My body, remembering the bodybuilding days, had good *muscle memory:* the ability to get back to a size you once were with less effort than those who hadn't gotten there before. Within a couple of months, I was noticing guys looking at me. They were wondering how I was able to put on a little bit of size when, after my three years of being away from the gym, they still looked the same as when I left. The hip and leg were slowly improving, and I knew, over time, an overall stronger body mass would allow me to work through and eliminate the pain. All I had to do was keep going. Slow and steady goes the race.

I had also added some yoga stretching to the end of my routine. As I lay on the mats, holding a pose, I noticed one of those foam tube rollers someone had left out on the mats. I remembered using one of those in the past. You would lie on top of it, such that it was below your hamstring, or thigh, or low back—whatever tight muscle group needed releasing—and with the weight of your body on top, roll back and forth pressing the tight muscles, as a rolling pin flattens out dough. I had an idea. My mind ran back to my acupressure training. Instead of stimulating each acupressure point, sometimes we used a rolling or rubbing technique to stimulate multiple points at the same time. "Maybe my pain has something to do with blocked Chi, and if I roll on those areas, it might resolve the pain that's been plaguing me for so long." Seemed reasonable, so I did. It felt pretty good. Very cool!

The next day, although there was some tenderness in the areas I'd rolled on, my hip and legs felt better! "Bonus! This is the solution! I'll keep doing this, from time to time, and I'll finally say goodbye to that unrelenting discomfort." Remember when I mentioned *"slow and steady goes the race"*? It went out the window and I decided to try it again—two days in a row. I rolled my right buttocks, hip, thigh, hamstring, and calf, as I had done the day before. The following morning, instead of feeling better, it felt worse—ten times worse! The pain was excruciating. I gobbled up Tylenol, hydromorphone, medical marijuana (I became a licensed user before being referred to the pain clinic), anything to numb the pain. I've had pain before, as you can imagine, but this pain was insurmountable. I went into panic mode, "There is no escape from this pain. When I lie down, it hurts. When I sit up, it hurts. Even when I stand, it hurts. It hurts! It hurts! It hurts! There was no escape! What am I going to do?" I was almost in tears. I hoped that it would subside, but it wouldn't.

"Get ready. I'm taking you to the hospital," Salome urged. "Do you think you need an ambulance?"

"Give me a minute," I requested. I lay back down in the bed. In one very specific position—just that one exact position—the pain seemed to subside. I lay there, not moving, long enough to gather the strength I'd need to put my clothes on and muster a quick clean up in the bathroom before attempting the stairs to go down to the main level. I hopped my way through it all; I could put no pressure on my right leg. It was winter, a week before Christmas, and after donning my coat and boots, I made my way to the car. Once inside, I quickly reclined the seat fully, and once again, took up that solitary position that relieved the pain. The hospital was only 15 minutes away, but it might as well have been in Timbuktu. I suffered through every bump, turn, and stoplight until we got there.

At the hospital, Salome had to run in to get someone to bring a gurney out, so that I could transfer from one reclining position to another in order to enter the emergency department. Unlike the luck I'd had in the past with ER admittances, once checked in, my gurney remained along a wall with a number of other poor souls waiting to be seen by a doctor. Thank goodness Salome, who worked at PRHC, spotted a co-worker friend who worked in the ER. We had already waited an hour, and although we didn't expect to jump the line ahead of anyone else, we wanted to know whether we were even in the queue. After a few moments, the co-worker came back to let us know that our paperwork was in a pile that caused it to get stalled, and she corrected the issue. Within moments we were taken to a curtain-clad stall, and then came the doctor.

After answering the typical barrage of questions, and explaining what had happened, the doctor gave us her opinion. "It looks like you've damaged your bursae, the fluid filled sacs that handle friction at the joints, and there's a lot of inflammation. Also, you rolled on your buttocks. It seems as though your sciatic nerve is being impinged as well." She left for a few moments then came back with two syringes: one with lidocaine to ease the pain, and the other with an anti-inflammatory she said wouldn't really kick in for about a week. We asked about immediate pain, and she said, "It's okay to continue with the hydromorphone and Tylenol—if you have more—but we don't prescribe that here," as she pointed up to a sign that read *The Emergency Department Does Not Prescribe Opioids*. "I'm also prescribing a rubbing compound you will need to get prepared at the pharmacy. Use it twice a day. Be prepared, this will take several weeks to heal." Then, in the blink of an eye, she was gone. Off to put out more fires.

The lidocaine blocked the nerves and numbed the region well enough that I could hobble to the ER entrance as Salome brought up the car. Thank heaven I was a drug minimalist. When I started feeling better after returning to the gym, I began weaning myself off the hydromorphone prescribed by the pain clinic. The extra pills I previously saved were invaluable in this emergency, because it was now the weekend and no way to contact the pain clinic for refills. Thank heaven for small mercies!

Back at home, I was bedridden for several weeks. I kept track of the daily ritual of rubbing compound, pain meds, transplant, and blood pressure meds. This process ran into the night and over the following week. My single resting and sleeping position slowly expanded into two, then three, then into multiple sleeping positions—almost resembling normal sleep. Still, at night, either the pain or the drugs caused me to sweat profusely. I'd wake up with my shirt and pillow soaked. I researched bursitis and found out that, quite often, the bursa become infected. "Maybe there's an infection that I am fighting? Why am I sweating so much? I wonder if there isn't something more happening here?" My mind was running wild with speculation. I thought of Denise, and how cancer had crept into her spinal cord and CSF; how she thought she had sciatica until she lost the use of her legs. "Was this happening to me? Was it my fate to go down that same road?" Possibly, it was the psychedelic effects of the drugs, because I usually didn't get so filled with fear about my own demise. Now it was on me, like the remora to the shark, clinging and nibbling away at my resolve.

I once asked a transplant team doctor, in the early days after T1, "What is it that causes a transplanted heart to fail? You hear about hearts lasting five years, sometimes ten years, sometimes more. What determines how long the organ will last? Does it just wear out?"

"It's usually heart disease or cancer," the doctor replied.

"Heart disease or cancer?" I contemplated. "I've never had issues with cholesterol (which I equated with heart disease)… And cancer? That's not for me. I've had this kidney thing, and this heart stuff, and that's my bailiwick, but I refuse to even think of cancer or get a cancer mentality. It's not going to happen!" Now, almost 20 years later, that same possibility of cancer was up in my face as a possible cause for my malaise. I couldn't get it out of my mind. "Would this problem become permanent? Would I become obsolete, or wheelchair-bound? Am I going to die from this, and leave my family behind? I can't even sit up for a few moments, enough to meditate. Everything is being taken away from me!"

On the night of December 26, as I lay in bed, I decided to do some distance reiki on myself. I'd planned on laying my hands on my hips, legs, and lower back areas on the right side, as I'd done several times over the past few days. Then, it came to me, I would have a much better outcome, and influence my deeper problem, if I undid the damage that was initially inflicted when I rolled those areas at the gym. I needed use the *distance* reiki symbol to journey back to the day I injured those body parts. As I felt the energy flowing through my hands, the hip area took in a lot of energy; I could feel it getting very hot, along with a strong pull through my hands. Although it was brief, as was most distance treatments, it was still very powerful!

The following night, just as I was falling asleep, I could feel myself needing to move—like I was being controlled by some benevolent force. My body pulled me in certain directions, then held positions, then moved again, and again. Intuitively, I could tell this pulling and contorting of my body was the result of the distance reiki treatment I had done the night before, sent out into the universe, and now it had returned. I started out laying prone beside Salome. I soon found myself hanging off the side of the bed, and in various strange positions directed by this energy, tightening and releasing, then directing me to the next position. As I'd typically done in the past, I mentally created a black hole, a vortex, to the right of myself and just down from the bed—a funnel to permanently throw off and discard any negative energies I no longer needed. This time, it seemed the contorting and pulling was drawing me down into the vortex. I was now completely off the bed, standing above the funnel. I could feel an etheric version of my body being dragged down into another dimension, so to speak. This etheric version felt as though it had traveled light years away, then returned to merge with my body, like the scout returning with information after reconnoitering. These programmed movements then brought me, piece by piece, back onto the bed. At times, I was bent in half with an arm dangling over the top of my head, then drawn back in the reverse direction. The reason for these movements and positions was unknown to me, yet they felt like prescribed positions, like spontaneous mudras; they had a purpose.

Next, was a period where I was seeing faces: the faces of women I'd had interactions with throughout my life. These interactions had been problematic for me but were also instructive for my development throughout life. Now, I was doing a review of all these personas, some I had not thought about for decades. It was as though I was doing an energetic apology to them all. Hugely emotional, yet silent. The movements then brought me back into the prone position beside Salome. My hand ended up in hers, and I somehow knew there would be some healing to do with, and for, her as well. As I held her, I sensed the deep feelings I had for her, tied with the gratitude I had for God, that he brought us together. Lastly, I had an image of the national and worldwide thought polarization of late; the endless differences of opinions, ending with people angry and raging at each other. This umbrella of healing now branched out to anyone who carried these negative emotions. I felt it very hard to breathe and gasped for air as I struggled to hold the energy for so many people. I knew I was being given the support and help from God, my guides, and Paramgurus[viii], in this vast, worthy effort. It was exhausting! Once it was completed, I passed out and had my first good night's sleep in weeks.

The next morning, I spent some time mulling over what had happened the night before. I would have questioned whether any of it was real, had I not seen many strange and amazing occurrences happen with clients on my own reiki table. I'd seen it all. Then, I realized, if I was my own client, I would have scanned the body to find out where the blockages were, then interpreted the blockages, which told a story about their life. In my case, I knew where the blockages were—right hip and right leg. The left side of the body is related to your *environment*, and the right side is related to your own thoughts, your will. This issue was about *my choices*. The hip represented your *role*—in society, your family, your environment—and the thigh and leg represented your *career* and the ease with which you step forward into it. Tying it all together, I realized that something was wrong with my role in society and that I wasn't stepping forward into my career with ease. I began asking myself, "What am I not doing that I am supposed to be doing?"

Then it came to me, like flapping up the dimly lit window blind to reveal the bright, blazing sun on a clear day. A promise I had made almost 20 years ago remained unfulfilled; a promise that was worth keeping me alive. I promised to share the story of my life to help others—to *be the example!* "It all makes sense!" I thought, "I can't believe I didn't catch on sooner. How could I have forgotten?" It's a common thing, for holistic practitioners to be so caught up in helping others, we forget to turn the searchlight of discrimination onto ourselves. Had I done so, I would've understood the meaning of my problems much sooner. I made a pact with God to save my life, and I never fulfilled it. Like he'd forget? He gently nudged me after my second heart transplant, using a little pain. Then again, with a little more. Over time, the nudges and the pain got stronger.

Until finally, God thought, "You're a stubborn one!" and brought the full pain of the right hip and leg to bear. That's when I heard Him. This was karma at its best. When most people think of karma, they think: *do something bad, get something bad back.* That's true, but there's also the karma of desire. If you desire things badly enough, you must get them. In my case, I did both. First, I desired my life to be extended. Therefore, I had to live long enough to receive that gift—whether in this life, or the next, I was to get an extended life.

You might think, "How is that bad? I'd like to live longer."

Don't forget, this life can be filled with suffering and pain. Desires make us *think* we want to stay on this earthly plane longer. When, after death, in the astral plane, we feel the bliss of God's presence; then, we want nothing more than to remain with Him. Escaping the wheel of rebirth, gives you the freedom to choose. Once free, you can choose to return to another life of struggle, or not. The choice becomes yours. "Hmmm…Live in bliss and joy versus pain and suffering. I choose bliss and joy every time."

Conversely, when you still have karma to pay, you have no choice. You are forced to return. The saying goes, "Be careful what you ask for," but it should be appended to say, "…and know *why* you're asking for it!"

Secondly, I made a promise to God. Then, I broke that promise. When I broke my promise to Him, I suffered, and continued to suffer, until I corrected it. Thankfully, I was getting back to an even keel of not creating any karma, and not repaying any karma. Let's keep it that way!

Once I began repaying my debt, all the fear of immobilization, cancer, sickness, all fell away. I no longer felt afraid. Every step I took in deciding how to make my pledge manifest eased my pain, little by little every day. I knew exactly how I'd heal my body: I'd write a book, a memoir, about the trials I've faced, intertwined with the realizations I made along the path. I would stand on a podium and speak to all those struggling with similar troubles, in the hopes that I can guide even one soul to salvation. I'd find a way to reach out to everyone—even you! In the meantime, *keep on roasting karma!* See you soon!

EPILOGUE

With equanimity, you can deal with situations with calm and reason while keeping your inner happiness.

~ The Dalai Lama

I hope you enjoyed my story. Truth is…the story continues: one scene merges with the next. At the time of writing this *Epilogue*, March 31, 2020, the world is sequestered away as the pandemic of COVID-19 plagues the globe. People struggle to stay indoors and adopt a new paradigm of social distancing forced upon them by global leaders. They fear for the future as financial markets crush their pensions and investments and as food and supplies vanish from the grocery store shelves. Is this the end? Not even close. Just a shuffling of the deck. Although not as severe, I was getting my kidney transplant smack dab in the middle of the SARS outbreak of 2002 and 2003. Being immune suppressed, it was dangerous to be in the hospital at that time. I survived it. As a species we survived it, and we'll survive this one too. The trick is surviving it and remaining whole; we must be able to smile and manifest happiness as the world around us constantly rearranges itself.

That was the purpose of writing *Roasting Karma*: to show that no matter how bad things get, we can train our inner thoughts to accept the good and the bad in equal measure. The Buddhists call it *equanimity*. When good things happen, it's easy to be peaceful or happy. When bad things happen, it's just as easy to be peaceful or happy—if we choose to be. Why would anyone choose to *not* be peaceful or happy? There could be many reasons, but the one that stands out most is because negative circumstances and events show up in our lives. Why do these situations show up? Quite often, the answer to that is karma. In the introduction to *Roasting Karma*, karma is defined as:

Karma is the law of action or cosmic justice, based upon cause and effect. Your every act, good or bad, has a specific effect on your life. The effects of actions in this life remain lodged in the subconsciousness; those brought over from past existences are hidden in the superconsciousness, ready like seeds to germinate under the influence of a suitable environment. Karma decrees that as one sows, so must he inevitably reap.

If every act, good or bad, has a specific effect on your life, and your actions have been recorded in your subconsciousness and superconsciousness over the course of lifetimes, it's very difficult to know why negative circumstances and events have shown up in your life. These things show up when the timing is right for you to learn from something you did in the past. Usually, when something shows up in our lives and we can't recall doing anything to deserve it; we find a way to blame the problem on someone else. Unfortunately, (once again from the introduction):

The blame game is a fruitless undertaking and only leads to sadness, anger, or guilt, for all parties involved—a lose-lose situation.

Then goes on to say:

Conversely, when we take responsibility for our actions, and then forgive ourselves, we cauterize those negative emotions and reveal a path through which happiness can flourish—win-win!

How does that work? It's all a matter of perspective. If we wade through life always feeling like we are being dumped on, or picked on, it's easy to end up with a *victim mentality*—a "people are always out to get me" attitude. When our own karma shows up—from our past or from past lives—that same victim mentality makes us think, "Here we go again. More problems being dumped on me that I didn't cause. Who is really to blame?" Then we blame someone else: a family member, a spouse, a friend, whoever is available. Quite often it's someone we already have a problem with, so we just throw our next issue into the mix, elevating the argument/battle to the next level. This behavior can also become habit-forming. Before we know it, this repeated scenario is running on autopilot and we stop thinking about our actions before engaging them. Someone does something to us and we lash back, automatically, without understanding why it was done to us in the first place—intentionally or unintentionally. As our habits and autonomic reactions continue over time, we get used to them and believe that, "It's just life. Get used to it!"

Thankfully, it's not *just life*. We don't have to live that way. Understanding that our previous actions, good or bad, have an impact on our lives moving forward, we have the ability to choose how we will respond to the repercussions of those past actions. We can decide which emotion to put forward— joy, peace, happiness—regardless of whether the repercussion is good or bad. Is it easy to do? No, but nothing is easy that's worth achieving. Just like graduating school or running a race: you had to study hard and/or practice every day but once you graduated or won, you never regretted the hard work that was put in to get there. You certainly don't regret the benefits that show up afterwards: a better job, an award, or an endorsement. The same goes here. We have to work on ourselves to stop being controlled by our habits, to be present and mindful of what is happening around us. It won't happen overnight, and it's a slow process, but we have to begin in order to get there.

What about horrible events that happen around us, like death, or murder, or rape? Are we supposed to smile and be happy when these events occur? Are we responsible for these events? To clarify, let me put it in another scenario. When we come into this life, we come alone. The events that happen around us can only be viewed by each of us individually and subjectively; no one can tell us what to think or feel. If an event occurs—someone spills a drink and it splashes on you—you are not responsible for the event taking place, but because you are involved, you are responsible for how you will respond to that event. Typically, if the person immediately said they were sorry and genuinely meant it, you would let it go, smile, and tell them it's okay. However, if that person was being careless and didn't apologize for the error, you might admonish that person to be more careful, or maybe just think, "What a jerk!" The trouble with this last approach is that you end up carrying those negative feelings around with you for the rest of the day. So, who's suffering? You are. The jerk is probably a jerk and never gave you a second thought. He freed himself from the event out of insensitivity, but you continue to carry it around with you. You may even get home, tell a friend or a family member, and wind them up, too. In other words, *you choose* to continue lugging the anchor of negative emotions around when the person who caused the problem let it go, long ago; maybe even right after it happened. Why suffer in this way?

So, let's go back to the death/murder/rape analogy. If you witness or experience grievous or heinous events, once again, *you are not responsible for the event taking place but because you are involved, you are responsible for how you will respond to the event.* As you've read, I was repeatedly subjected to invasive procedures as I lay exposed and vulnerable, I've experienced the death of close family members, and, as a person of color, I've been the subject of unprovoked racial attacks (not mentioned in the book)—and I reacted! I reacted to all of them, sometimes vehemently, but came to realize carrying that anger, frustration, grief, or shame around wasn't going to make things any better. I had to let them go. Likewise, when you see these types of events happening to others, accordingly, you would offer the appropriate acknowledgment—condolences or empathy—but inside you can remain unshaken. You offer the acknowledgement as an act of kindness for another human being, but it isn't necessary to suffer unendingly because of your life experiences. That's what I mean when I say you can take responsibility for the things that happen in your life.

Taking responsibility for life's events with equanimity and choosing love-based emotions over fear-based emotions is a cyclical process that feeds upon itself. When we consider the Law of Attraction and what we focus on becomes our reality, we soon find more equanimity and more love-based emotions showing up in our lives. Add in a little meditation to slow the onslaught of thoughts that preoccupy our minds, and we are more able to free ourselves from the habits that keep us operating on autopilot. This is the recipe for a more peaceful life.

In writing *Roasting Karma,* and more specifically this epilogue, I've come to realize that while many can see reflections of themselves in the pages of my story and have a desire to change their lives toward peace and happiness, they may need some guidance in getting there. After all, I learned the process over a span of approximately 20 years. I've done the heavy lifting and would like to make the process easier for you. I'm in the process of preparing a companion workbook to help anyone interested in doing their own personal work. Look for *Roast Your Own Karma* coming soon.

I roast karma because I'd like to free myself from the wheel of rebirth, or reincarnation. You may hear people say, "This is my last time on this earth. I've evolved. I'm not coming back again!" That may be all well and good, and they may truly believe that they won't have to come back, but unless they have paid back all their karma, they will be back again. That's the way it works. That's why I make every effort to take on my own karma with equanimity and a smile on my face because in my humble opinion, nothing is more important. Keep on roasting karma!

PHOTO GALLERY

1968 – Kirk, age 3, with his mother, B. R. (Joy) Johnson, at the Olac Baby Contest in Kingston, Jamaica. Baby Kirk won first place.

1972 – Kirk, age 7, Grade 2 school photo, Kitchener, Ontario.

1977 – Kirk, age 12, with his father, Welsey S. Johnson, at their home in Country Hills, Kitchener, Ontario.

1984 – Kirk, age 19, with his Eastwood Collegiate Track & Field teammates, Kitchener, Ontario.

1988 – Kirk, age 23, competing at the Tournament of Champions, heavyweight division (Ontario amateur bodybuilding). Placed second in the division.

1989 – Kirk, age 24, holding newborn son, Travis Anthony Johnson, at home in Kitchener, Ontario.

1990 – My mother, Joy (in long dress), and my sisters (L-R), Donna, Paula, and Allison, in Toronto, Ontario,

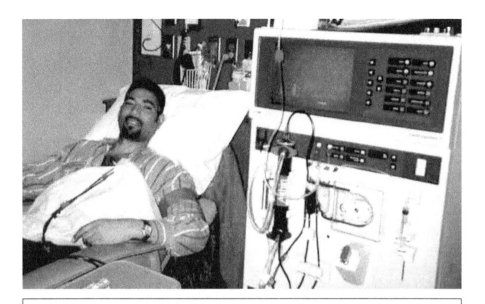

1998 – Kirk, age 33, first dialysis session in Oshawa, Ontario. No dialysis spots available in Peterborough. Had to travel 45 minutes, three times a week, to get treatment.

1999 – Kirk, age 34, with 6-month old Nathaniel James Johnson at their home in Peterborough, Ontario. This photo is three months prior to Kirk's full-time hospitalization in Toronto to wait for his transplants.

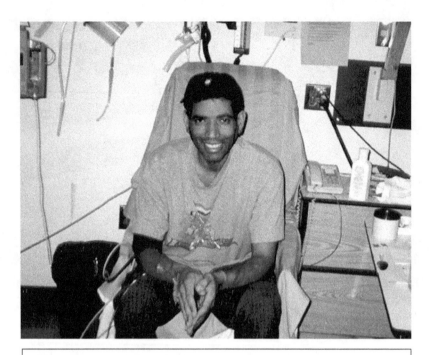

2000 – Kirk, age 35, waiting for heart and kidney transplants at Mount Sinai Hospital in Toronto, Ontario. He lost a lot of weight, going from 230 pounds down to 175, a mere shadow of his former self.

2003 – Kirk, age 38, three years after first heart transplant and six months after kidney transplant, at his home is Peterborough, Ontario. Back to a normal weight of 220 pounds.

2002 – Kirk, age 37, with wife Lorie, sons Travis (top) and Nathaniel in Peterborough, Ontario. Lorie had recently completed chemotherapy and related breast cancer surgeries.

2007 – Kirk, age 42, with Nathan at their Twin Sisters Lakes cottage in Ontario. Kirk had already received his kidney transplant. Lorie passed away the previous year.

2004 – Kirk, age 39, receives the Master-level Reiki attunement from Reiki Master, Bernard Morin, beside the Atlantic Ocean in Newfoundland, Canada.

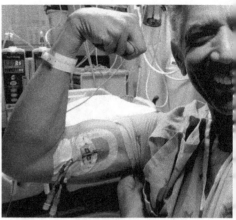

2015 – Kirk, revisited Panama for his 50th birthday. Denise had returned to Panama after receiving chemotherapy for breast cancer. She passed away in August, back in Peterborough, Ontario.

2016 – Kirk, age 51, at Toronto General Hospital getting a heart tune-up and doing the work-up for a second heart transplant.

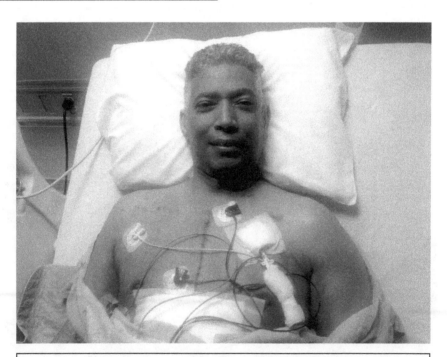

2017 – Kirk, age 52, at Toronto General Hospital after receiving his second heart transplant. Morphine is a wonderful thing!

2017 – Kirk, age 52, with Salome Shyan (later Johnson) at Starbucks in Toronto prior to a follow-up biopsy, one month after his second heart transplant.

2019 – Kirk, age 54, forced to recline for Christmas after damaging his hip bursae. He is surrounded by (top to bottom) Nathan, Phoebe Bergeron and Misha Bergeron (stepdaughter and stepson). It was a great Christmas.

ABOUT THE AUTHOR

Kirk Johnson is a two-time heart and kidney transplant survivor. While waiting for his first heart transplant in 2000, Kirk asked himself, "Why should I be kept alive over anybody else?" The answer came to him in deep meditation. If he were to become an example for others to follow when in the pit of despair, he would be worthy of a second chance. Kirk was given a second chance and is using his personal, real-life experiences to help others through his writing, speaking, teaching, and mentoring.

A Jamaican-born Canadian living in Canada since the age of three, Kirk brings with him a wealth of information on surviving life's trials, as well as extensive holistic therapy experience. He is an Acupressure Therapist, Reiki Master, Holistic Body Analysis Practitioner, Spiritual Mentor, and an ordained metaphysical minister. He also practices Kriya yoga meditation, twice daily, and has done so for 15 years. He and his wife, Salome, live outside Toronto, Ontario, and share four amazing children: Travis, Nathaniel, Misha, and Phoebe.

Kirk has helped numerous individuals resolve health issues, as well as find peace and balance through his holistic practices in Canada and the Republic of Panama, where he operated a satellite practice for a number of years. He developed a multitier approach: first solving problems on the material level using diet, herbs, and supplements; then if problems persist, he works using energetic and vibrational means; and if the problems still persist, he works using more spiritual or esoteric therapies. He is known as the practitioner who doesn't let anyone *escape* from doing their work. He works closely with his clients to help them *go deep* to resolve the roots of their *dis-ease*.

Connect with Kirk: kirkajohnson.com

Your Next Steps with Roasting Karma:

- Yes, I saw myself in this book.
- Yes, I want to become more awake.
- Yes, I'd like to know how to take my life to the next level.
- Yes, I'm open to new ways of transformation.

Start:

RoastingKarma.com

Today!

ENDNOTES

i   Glossary and Pronunciation Guide. (n.d.). Retrieved June 3, 2020, from https://yogananda.org/self-realization-fellowship-glossary#R-S

ii   Paramahansa Yogananda Quotes on Karma. (n.d.). Retrieved June 3, 2020, from http://yogananda.com.au/gurus/yoganandaquotes06c.html

iii   Revelation 3.12 NKJV. (n.d.). Retrieved June 3, 2020, from https://www.bible.com/bible/114/REV.3.12.NKJV

iv   About Kriya Yoga. (n.d.). Retrieved June 3, 2020, from https://anandapune.org/meditation-kriya-yoga/

v   Glossary and Pronunciation Guide. (n.d.-b). Retrieved June 3, 2020, from https://yogananda.org/self-realization-fellowship-glossary#R-S

vi   Wikipedia contributors. (2020). Master T. Retrieved June 3, 2020, from https://en.wikipedia.org/wiki/Master_T

vii   Ejection Fraction Heart Failure Measurement. (2017, May 31). Retrieved June 3, 2020, from https://www.heart.org/en/health-topics/heart-failure/diagnosing-heart-failure/ejection-fraction-heart-failure-measurement

viii   Paramaguru. (n.d.). Retrieved June 3, 2020, from https://www.yogapedia.com/definition/5830/paramaguru

CPSIA information can be obtained
at www.ICGtesting.com
Printed in the USA
BVHW031054290920
589808BV00001B/5